THE CUMBRIA AND LAKE DISTRICT COAST

A guide to places to visit, history and wildlife from Morecambe Bay to the Solway Firth

Kevin Sene

Copyright © 2021 Kevin Sene

The moral right of the author has been asserted

Apart from any fair dealing for the purposes of research or private study, or criticism or review, as permitted under the Copyright, Designs and Patents Act 1988, this publication may only be reproduced, stored or transmitted, in any form or by any means, with the prior permission in writing of the publishers, or in the case of reprographic reproduction in accordance with the terms of licences issued by the Copyright Licensing Agency. Enquiries concerning reproduction outside those terms should be sent to the publishers.

Matador
9 Priory Business Park
Wistow Road, Kibworth Beauchamp
Leicestershire, LE8 0RX
Tel: 0116 279 2299
Email: books@troubador.co.uk
Web: www.troubador.co.uk/matador
Twitter: @matadorbooks

ISBN: 9781800464049

All photographs © Kevin Sene unless otherwise stated.

Maps contain Ordnance Survey data © Crown copyright and database right (2021). Maps are indicative only; please refer to original OS maps for more details.

British Library Cataloguing in Publication Data.
A catalogue record for this book is available from the British Library.

Printed and bound by CPI Group (UK) Ltd, Croydon, CR0 4YY

Matador is an imprint of Troubador Publishing Ltd.

MIX
Paper from
responsible sources
FSC
www.fsc.org FSC® C013604

IMPORTANT ADVICE
Although the author and publisher have taken all reasonable care in preparing this guide, we make no explicit guarantees as to the accuracy or completeness of the information and advice contained and cannot accept any responsibility for any accident, injury, trespass, inconvenience, loss or damage from its use. Before travelling, readers should check opening times and travel details and note that all outdoor activities are at their own risk and require a reasonable level of fitness; see later in this chapter for safety tips. We would be grateful to know of any errors or out-of-date information.

THE CUMBRIA AND LAKE DISTRICT COAST

Acknowledgements

Author, design and layout: Kevin Sene
www.meteowriter.com
Copy editing: Helen Fazal
Cover Design: Jack Wedgbury
Front cover: Maryport Harbour (2014)
Frontispiece: Leven Estuary
Previous page: Guillemots at St Bees Head
Cartography: Kevin Sene
Maps contain OS data © Crown copyright and database right (2021)
Typesetting: Joe Shillito

About the author

Kevin Sene is a scientist and writer on water and climate themes. The idea for this guide arose from many enjoyable walks and cycle rides around the Cumbrian coast when living in Kendal and Carlisle and an interest in its wildlife and tidal bores. He has also written a travel guide to the Mersey Estuary and its Liverpool, Wirral and Cheshire shores; see www.meteowriter.com for details. He is a Fellow of the Royal Geographical Society and has worked extensively in Europe, Africa and Asia.

Credits

All photographs are by the author, taken on many enjoyable trips over the years, except for the following images:

- Bay Search & Rescue — 20
- Conishead Priory — 96
- Cumbria Wildlife Trust — 87
- Doc Searls — 57
- Dr Bruce G Marcot — 155
- Lakeland Motor Museum — 94
- Lakeside and Haverthwaite Railway — 93
- Lancaster Museums — 81
- The Beacon Museum — 36
- The Dock Museum — 106
- U.S. Fish and Wildlife Service — 45

Much has been written about the Lake District and Cumbria and the Further Reading section at the end of the book notes publications and websites that were particularly useful. Interpretation panels at museums, nature reserves and tourist attractions were other useful sources of information. Where possible, original sources are cited, although we apologise if there have been any unintentional errors.

Thanks also to representatives from the following organisations, sites and projects who kindly provided comments on short excerpts of text:

- Arnside and Silverdale AONB
- Bay Search & Rescue
- Caerlaverock Wetland Centre
- Carnforth Station Heritage Centre
- Conishead Priory
- Cumbria Wildlife Trust
- Devil's Porridge Museum
- Dumfries Museum
- Dynamic Dunescapes
- Foulshaw Moss Nature Reserve
- Guide over Sands Trust
- Lake District Coast Aquarium
- Lake District National Park Authority
- Lakeland Motor Museum
- Lakeside and Haverthwaite Railway
- Lancaster Canal Trust
- Lancaster Maritime Museum
- Millom Heritage & Arts Centre
- Ravenglass & Eskdale Railway
- RNLI
- RSPB
- Sea Watch Foundation
- Senhouse Roman Museum
- Solway Coast AONB
- South Walney Nature Reserve
- The Beacon Museum
- The Dock Museum
- The Rum Story
- Tullie House Museum & Art Gallery

Thanks also to Gill Jepson for comments on the text on Furness Abbey, Dave Blackledge for comments on the text on the RSPB's Cumbrian coastal reserves, Jane Tyler and Peter Smart for help with bird identification, and Lindsay Martindale for help with proof reading.

> For more information on this book and others by the author, please see www.meteowriter.com. This includes links to higher resolution versions of selected photographs for editorial and personal use. If you have found this book useful and would like to leave a review, please consider using Goodreads (www.goodreads.com) or the retailer's website.

INTRODUCTION	1

About this guide	5	Getting around	15
When to visit	12	Water safety	20
Tourist information	14		

1. COASTAL THEMES	25

Habitat	26	Wildlife	43
Maritime History	32		

2. MORECAMBE BAY	55

Lancashire shores	59	Leven Estuary and Furness Peninsula	91
Kent Estuary	71		

3. IRISH SEA	115

Irish Sea coast	119	Ravenglass Estuary	139
Duddon Estuary	123		

4. SOLWAY FIRTH	153

Cumbria shores	157	Scottish shores	187

FURTHER READING	195
INDEX	198

A fishing trawler leaving Whitehaven viewed from above the Beacon Museum

INTRODUCTION

The Cumbrian coastline extends from Morecambe Bay to the Solway Firth with several major estuaries along its shores.

The views change appearance with the ebb and flow of the tides, providing great walking and photographic opportunities, often with distant Lake District fells as a scenic backdrop.

Sailing ships and coastal steamers once plied these waters and there are still several busy ports, although most are now home to fishing fleets and leisure craft. Reminders of this seafaring past include lighthouses, piers and a ruined fort.

In the winter, sandbanks and mudflats attract large numbers of wading birds, which sometimes form spectacular flocks as they move inland with the rising tide. Seals, ospreys and seabirds are other highlights.

Several museums celebrate the maritime history and wildlife of the region. Other great places to visit include stately homes, nature reserves and seaside resorts.

REGIONAL SUMMARY

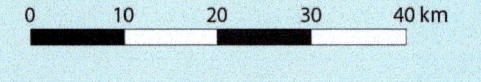

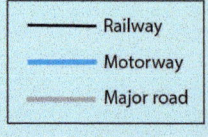

DUMFRIES & GALLOWAY

Wigtown

Mull of Galloway

0		10		20		30		40 km

- Railway
- Motorway
- Major road

Maps are indicative only and contain OS data
© Crown copyright and database right (2021)

Map of Cumbria and the Lake District

Scotland / Cumbria region:
- Dumfries
- Annan
- Gretna
- A74 (M)
- Bowness-on-Solway
- Cardurnock Peninsula
- Silloth
- Carlisle
- Allonby

Solway Firth

CUMBRIA

West Coast:
- Maryport
- Workington
- Whitehaven
- St Bees
- Egremont
- Seascale
- Ravenglass
- Ravenglass Estuary

Irish Sea

Lake District:
- Keswick
- LAKE DISTRICT NATIONAL PARK
- Ennerdale Water
- Brockhole on Windermere
- Bowness on Windermere
- Windermere
- Kendal
- M6

South:
- Millom
- Duddon Estuary
- Ulverston
- Cark
- Grange-over-Sands
- Arnside
- Milnthorpe
- Leven Estuary
- Kent Estuary
- Carnforth
- Walney Island
- Morecambe
- Lancaster
- Lune Estuary
- Fleetwood

Morecambe Bay

LANCASHIRE

Introduction

The coastline of Cumbria is hugely varied with seaside resorts, nature reserves and historic towns. The nearby Lakeland hills are often fine viewpoints and the many west-facing shores give the chance to see spectacular sunsets.

Several long-distance walks begin at the coast, including the Coast to Coast Path and Hadrian's Wall Path. The England Coast Path is increasingly attracting walkers to these shores.

Estuaries are a particular feature, accounting for more than half of the Cumbrian coastline and strongly influencing its history and wildlife. Situated at the margins of the land where rivers meet the sea, for centuries they have provided a convenient shipping route inland and were a natural place to build ports and harbours. Many of these settlements have a fascinating maritime history, in some cases stretching from Roman times to the wealth built on iron and coal during the industrial revolution.

Navigation was not without its challenges due to the funnelling effect as the tide rushes in, leading to strong currents and some of the highest tidal ranges in the world. On the highest tides, amazing waves called tidal bores occur on several estuaries, often breaking into a line of surf.

Extensive areas of sand and mud are then exposed as the tide goes out. During medieval times, these provided a shortcut for travellers and in the 19th century there was even a scheduled stagecoach service across Morecambe Bay. Nowadays, only the foolhardy would risk these crossings without an experienced guide, but guided charity walks are popular, led by the Queen's Guide to the Sands.

> **STAY SAFE!**
> Around the coast and estuaries in this guide, there are risks from the tides and from soft mud and quicksand, even when strolling along the beach. The Royal National Lifeboat Institution (RNLI) publishes some excellent advice on water safety, which is reproduced later in this chapter (www.rnli.org). In addition to checking tide times, it is worth checking if any flood alerts or warnings are in force for areas you plan to visit (www.gov.uk).

The harbour at Maryport at low tide ▼

INTRODUCTION | 5

The sands and mudflats are also rich with shellfish, worms and other prey, which in winter attract large numbers of wading birds. These provide great birdwatching and photographic opportunities as do the lowland peat bogs or mires along estuary shores. Once much more extensive, most of the remaining mires are now protected, providing food and shelter for insects and birds.

Other dramatic wildlife includes ospreys in the Kent Estuary, a seal colony in Morecambe Bay, and seabirds nesting on spectacular cliffs in the Solway Firth. Many nature reserves dot these shores along with two more extensive Areas of Outstanding Natural Beauty: the Arnside and Silverdale AONB in the south and the Solway Coast AONB in the north.

▲ Furness Abbey, near Barrow-in-Furness, was one of the most powerful in the region in medieval times

About this guide

This guide is about places to visit around the coast of the Lake District and Cumbria and its history and wildlife. It will be of interest to local residents and visitors alike. Topics include:

- Places to visit: museums, stately homes, viewpoints, tourist attractions
- Maritime history: the Roman occupation, lighthouses, ports, harbours, canals
- Wildlife: habitat, ospreys, salmon, wading birds, nature reserves

Source to sea summaries describe the rivers that flow down from the Lake District fells. The Lancashire shores of Morecambe Bay are considered, too, along with the Scottish shores of the Solway Firth.

▲ The stately home of Muncaster Castle near Ravenglass in west Cumbria

▲ A flock of oystercatchers near the RSPB's Campfield Marsh reserve on the Solway Firth

GOOD PLACES FOR LOCAL AND MARITIME HISTORY
- Fleetwood Museum (Morecambe Bay)
- Lancaster Maritime Museum (Morecambe Bay)
- The Dock Museum, Barrow-in-Furness (Morecambe Bay)
- Millom Heritage & Arts Centre (Duddon Estuary)
- The Beacon Museum, Whitehaven (Solway Firth)
- The Rum Story, Whitehaven (Solway Firth)
- Maryport Maritime Museum (Solway Firth)
- Tullie House Museum & Art Gallery, Carlisle (Solway Firth)
- Annan Museum (Solway Firth)
- Dumfries Museum (Solway Firth)

GOOD PLACES FOR A BIRD'S EYE VIEW
- Williamson Park, Lancaster (Morecambe Bay)
- Arnside Knott (Kent Estuary)
- Hampsfell (Kent Estuary)
- Humphrey Head (Kent Estuary)
- Sir John Barrow Monument, Ulverston (Leven Estuary)
- Dunnerholme (Duddon Estuary)
- Black Combe (Duddon Estuary, Irish Sea)
- Newtown Knott (Ravenglass Estuary)
- Binsey, Cumbria (Solway Firth)
- Criffel, Dumfries and Galloway (Solway Firth)

GOOD PLACES FOR MARITIME CONNECTIONS
- Plover Scar Lighthouse (Morecambe Bay)
- St George's Quay, Lancaster (Morecambe Bay)
- Arnside Pier (Kent Estuary)
- Canal Foot, Ulverston (Leven Estuary)
- Piel Island (Morecambe Bay)
- Walney Lighthouse (Morecambe Bay)
- Hodbarrow Lighthouse (Duddon Estuary)
- St Bees Lighthouse (Solway Firth)
- Port Carlisle (Solway Firth)
- Mull of Galloway (Solway Firth)

GOOD PLACES FOR SEASIDE VISITS
- Fleetwood (Morecambe Bay)
- Morecambe (Morecambe Bay)
- Arnside (Kent Estuary)
- Grange-over-Sands (Kent Estuary)
- Haverigg (Duddon Estuary)
- Silecroft (Irish Sea)
- Seascale (Irish Sea)
- St Bees (Irish Sea)
- Allonby (Solway Firth)
- Silloth (Solway Firth)

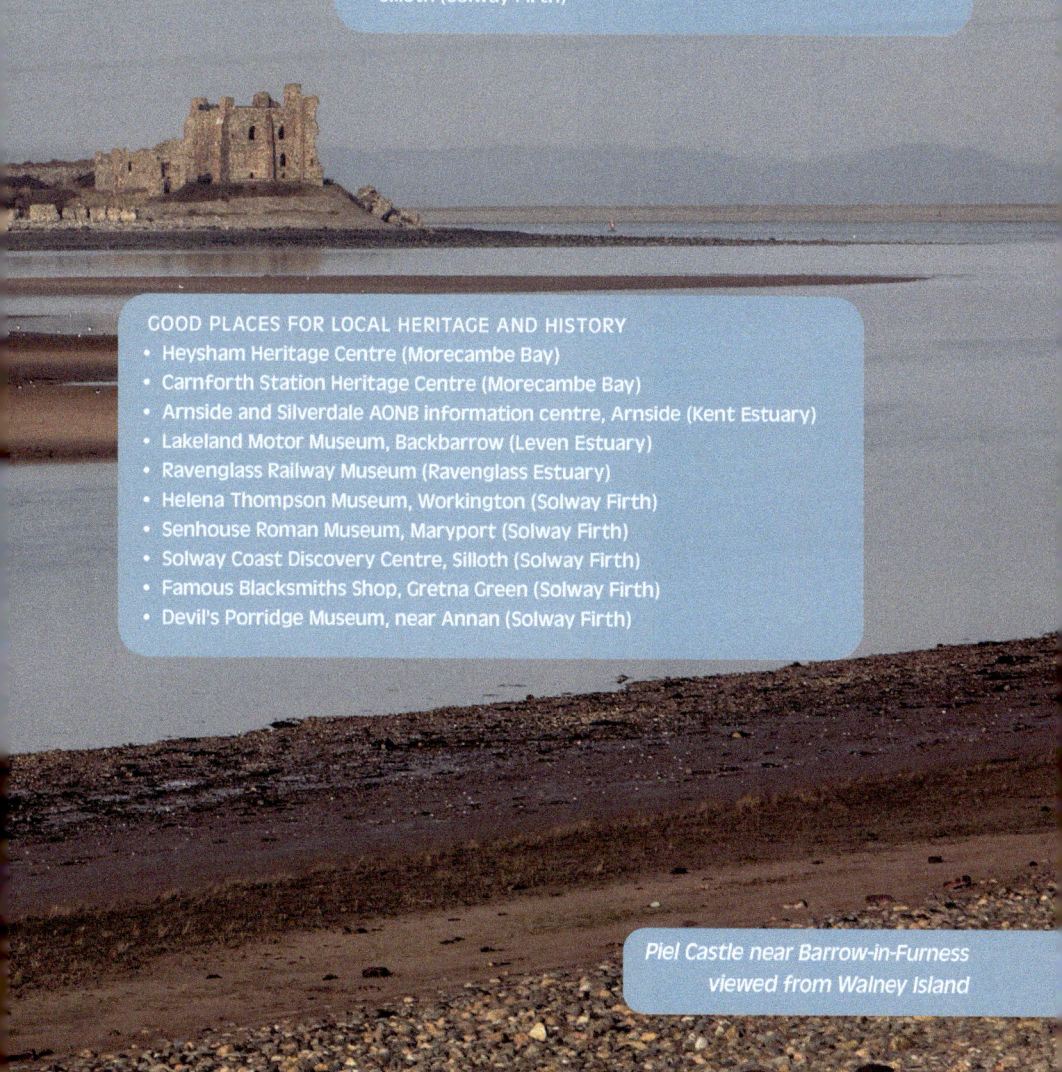

GOOD PLACES FOR LOCAL HERITAGE AND HISTORY
- Heysham Heritage Centre (Morecambe Bay)
- Carnforth Station Heritage Centre (Morecambe Bay)
- Arnside and Silverdale AONB information centre, Arnside (Kent Estuary)
- Lakeland Motor Museum, Backbarrow (Leven Estuary)
- Ravenglass Railway Museum (Ravenglass Estuary)
- Helena Thompson Museum, Workington (Solway Firth)
- Senhouse Roman Museum, Maryport (Solway Firth)
- Solway Coast Discovery Centre, Silloth (Solway Firth)
- Famous Blacksmiths Shop, Gretna Green (Solway Firth)
- Devil's Porridge Museum, near Annan (Solway Firth)

Piel Castle near Barrow-in-Furness viewed from Walney Island

GOOD PLACES FOR WILDLIFE
- Leighton Moss (Morecambe Bay)
- Arnside Knott (Kent Estuary)
- Foulshaw Moss (Kent Estuary)
- Foulney Island (Morecambe Bay)
- South Walney Island (Morecambe Bay)
- Hodbarrow (Duddon Estuary)
- St Bees Head (Solway Firth)
- Campfield Marsh (Solway Firth)
- Caerlaverock (Solway Firth)
- Mersehead (Solway Firth)

GOOD PLACES FOR HISTORIC BUILDINGS
- Levens Hall (Kent Estuary)
- Cartmel Priory (Kent Estuary)
- Holker Hall (Leven Estuary)
- Conishead Priory (Leven Estuary)
- Duddon Iron Furnace (Duddon Estuary)
- Muncaster Castle (Ravenglass Estuary)
- St Bees Priory (Irish Sea)
- St Michael's Church, Burgh by Sands (Solway Firth)
- Holme Cultram Abbey (Solway Firth)
- Sweetheart Abbey (Solway Firth)

GOOD PLACES FOR ANCIENT SITES
- St Patrick's Chapel, Heysham (Morecambe Bay)
- Birkrigg Stone Circle (Leven Estuary)
- Furness Abbey (Morecambe Bay)
- Piel Castle (Morecambe Bay)
- Swinside Stone Circle (Duddon Estuary)
- Roman Bath House (Ravenglass Estuary)
- Roman fort remains, Maryport (Solway Firth)
- Milefortlet 21 (Solway Firth)
- Crosscanonby Saltpans (Solway Firth)
- King Edward I Monument, Burgh by Sands (Solway Firth)

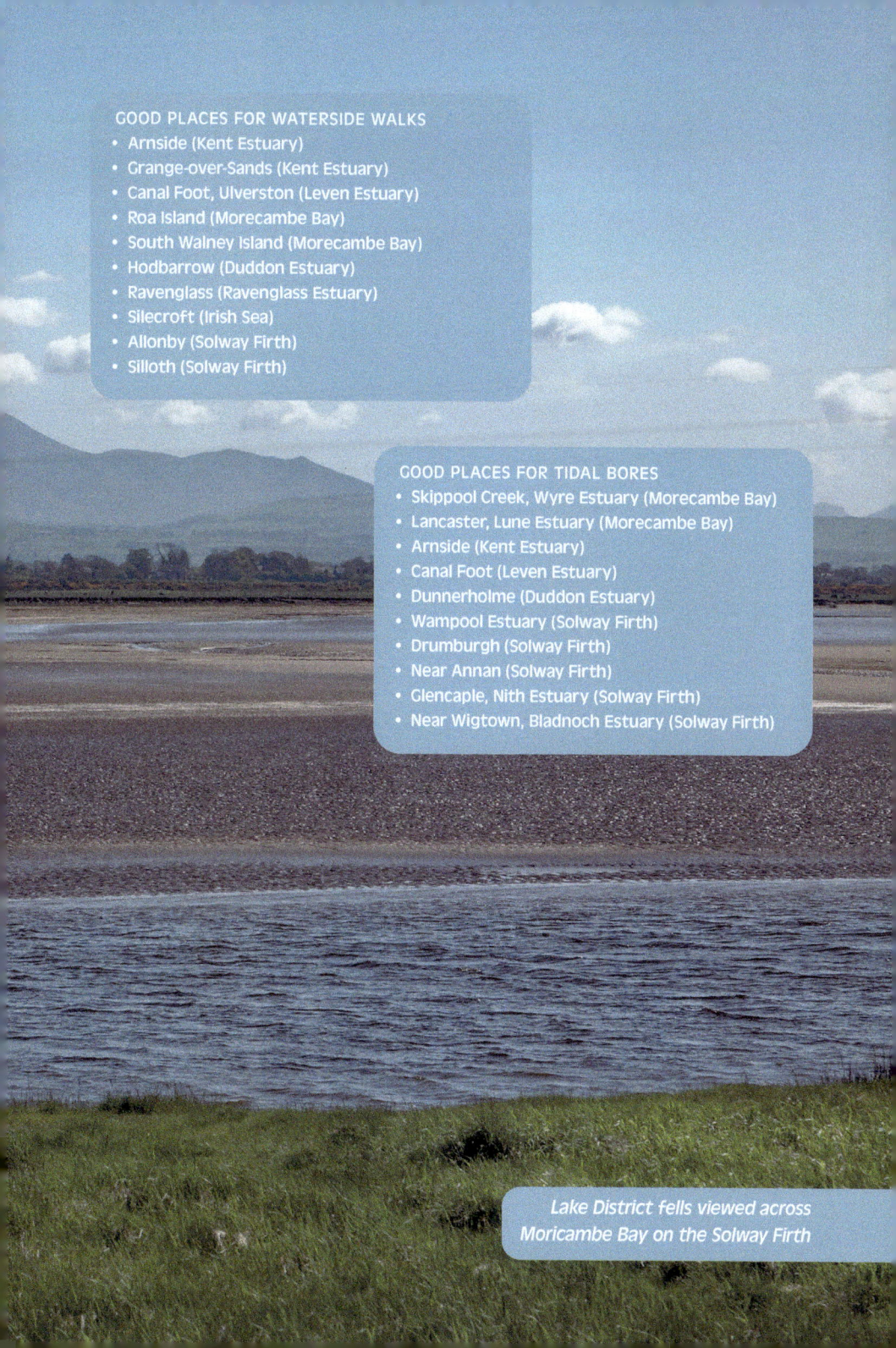

GOOD PLACES FOR WATERSIDE WALKS
- Arnside (Kent Estuary)
- Grange-over-Sands (Kent Estuary)
- Canal Foot, Ulverston (Leven Estuary)
- Roa Island (Morecambe Bay)
- South Walney Island (Morecambe Bay)
- Hodbarrow (Duddon Estuary)
- Ravenglass (Ravenglass Estuary)
- Silecroft (Irish Sea)
- Allonby (Solway Firth)
- Silloth (Solway Firth)

GOOD PLACES FOR TIDAL BORES
- Skippool Creek, Wyre Estuary (Morecambe Bay)
- Lancaster, Lune Estuary (Morecambe Bay)
- Arnside (Kent Estuary)
- Canal Foot (Leven Estuary)
- Dunnerholme (Duddon Estuary)
- Wampool Estuary (Solway Firth)
- Drumburgh (Solway Firth)
- Near Annan (Solway Firth)
- Glencaple, Nith Estuary (Solway Firth)
- Near Wigtown, Bladnoch Estuary (Solway Firth)

Lake District fells viewed across Moricambe Bay on the Solway Firth

WHAT IS AN ESTUARY?

As a river approaches the coast, water levels start to be affected by the tides. The point where this occurs is often considered to be the start of an estuary. On Ordnance Survey 1:25 000 scale maps it is marked by NTL, which stands for Normal Tidal Limit.

Even in hilly Cumbria, the tidal limit is sometimes many miles inland, such as on the Kent, Leven and Duddon estuaries. It is just a typical value, though, and on the highest tides can extend further upstream, sometimes leading to flooding of roads and properties.

The wide expanses of Morecambe Bay and the Solway Firth are often thought of as estuaries although at their seaward margins there is little to distinguish them from open sea. However, closer to the shore large areas of mudflats and sandbanks appear at low tide.

▲ Sandbanks on the Kent Estuary viewed at low tide from Arnside Knott

The word *firth* has the same root as the Norwegian word *fjord*, which is a sea inlet or an arm of the sea. For the Solway Firth, Scottish Government publications refer to the uppermost reaches as the Solway Estuary. This is based on a widely used definition for where an estuary ends, which is the point at which seawater is no longer diluted by fresh water from rivers and streams. Again, this is not a precise location and is open to some interpretation.

Another feature of the Cumbrian coastline is the large difference in water levels between low and high tide. This difference, known as the tidal range, is one of the highest in the UK, in places exceeding ten metres on the highest tides.

This creates some great photographic opportunities as the browns and greens of sandbanks, mudflats and saltmarsh give way to open water, but presents a risk, and the lifeboat services around the coastline often have to rescue people caught out by the tides. Some RNLI tips on water safety appear later and are essential reading.

INTRODUCTION | 11

This **Introduction** gives practical information to help when visiting the area, including ideas for when to visit, how to get around, where to find information on travel and accommodation, and water safety. Top-ten listings give a handy summary of suggestions for places to visit.

A chapter on **Coastal themes** gives insights into maritime history and wildlife. This discusses coastal settlement since the last Ice Age, how the estuaries formed, and the types of bird and marine life found around their shores. There are also tips on how to find out tide times, with an introduction to how tidal bores form.

The coastline is then considered in three separate chapters. The first describes **Morecambe Bay**, including the two estuaries that stretch along its Cumbrian shores, the Kent Estuary and

▲ A tidal bore on the Duddon Estuary

FIX THE FELLS
The Lake District fells are rightly one of the UK's most popular hillwalking destinations, but this places pressure on footpaths, affecting landscapes and wildlife. Fix the Fells is working to reduce these problems and as their website says 'We are a team of skilled rangers and volunteers who repair and maintain the mountain paths in the Lake District with funding from donations and partners. A combination of millions of pairs of walking boots, the weather and gradient means erosion is a constant problem. Our path work reduces erosion scars and also helps protect the ecology and archaeological heritage of our beautiful landscape.' See www.fixthefells.co.uk to find out more, including how to support this work.

THE LAKE DISTRICT NATIONAL PARK
The Lake District National Park was established in 1951 and covers an area of 912 square miles. It encompasses most of the high mountains and lakes of Cumbria and twenty-six miles of coastline and estuaries. This includes the uppermost reaches of the Kent and the Leven estuaries, although only the Ravenglass Estuary lies entirely within the national park.

In 2016 the boundary of the park was extended eastwards to meet the Yorkshire Dales National Park in an area north of Kendal. The following year the English Lake District was designated as a UNESCO World Heritage Site, joining other fabulous destinations such as the Taj Mahal in India, the Great Pyramid of Giza and, more locally, Hadrian's Wall.

the Leven Estuary. Towns and villages here include Arnside, Grange-over-Sands, Ulverston and Barrow-in-Furness. Tourist destinations on its Lancashire shores are discussed too, including Fleetwood, Lancaster and Morecambe.

An **Irish Sea** chapter then looks at the coastline in southwest Cumbria and the two main estuaries along its shores. These are the Duddon Estuary, where the largest town is Millom, and the Ravenglass Estuary, at the meeting place of three rivers that begin near Scafell Pike, the highest peak in the Lake District. Other sights along the coastline include the Victorian coastal resort of Seascale and the historic town of St Bees.

The final chapter focuses on the **Solway Firth**. This stretches from St Bees in Cumbria to the Mull of Galloway in Scotland and includes the towns of Whitehaven, Workington, Maryport and Silloth. The city of Carlisle is considered, too, and destinations along its Scottish shores, including Gretna, Annan, Dumfries and Wigtown.

A **Further Reading** section suggests books, reports and websites that that may be of interest, including some that were particularly useful when researching this guide.

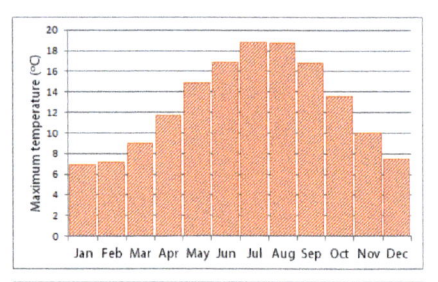

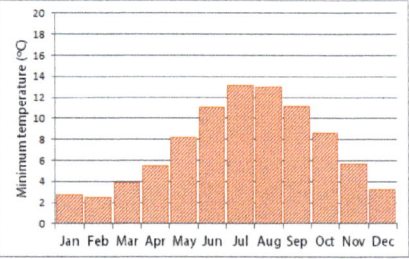

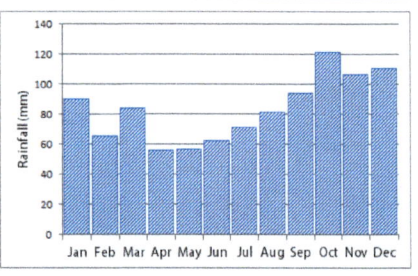

▲ Monthly average maximum and minimum air temperatures and monthly average rainfall for the Met Office meteorological station at Walney Island in the period 1981 to 2010 (data from www.metoffice.gov.uk. Contains public sector information licensed under the Open Government Licence v1.0)

(Top) Festival in Carlisle ▶
(Bottom) Winter views near the Kent Estuary ▶

When to visit

Due to its mountainous terrain, the Lake District is famed for its ever-changing weather, which in places leads to some of the highest rainfall in the UK.

Around the coast, the weather tends to be less extreme, and it may even be dry when it is raining or snowing inland. For example, the average annual rainfall at Ambleside, at just 60 metres above sea level, is almost double that at St Bees Head on the western coast.

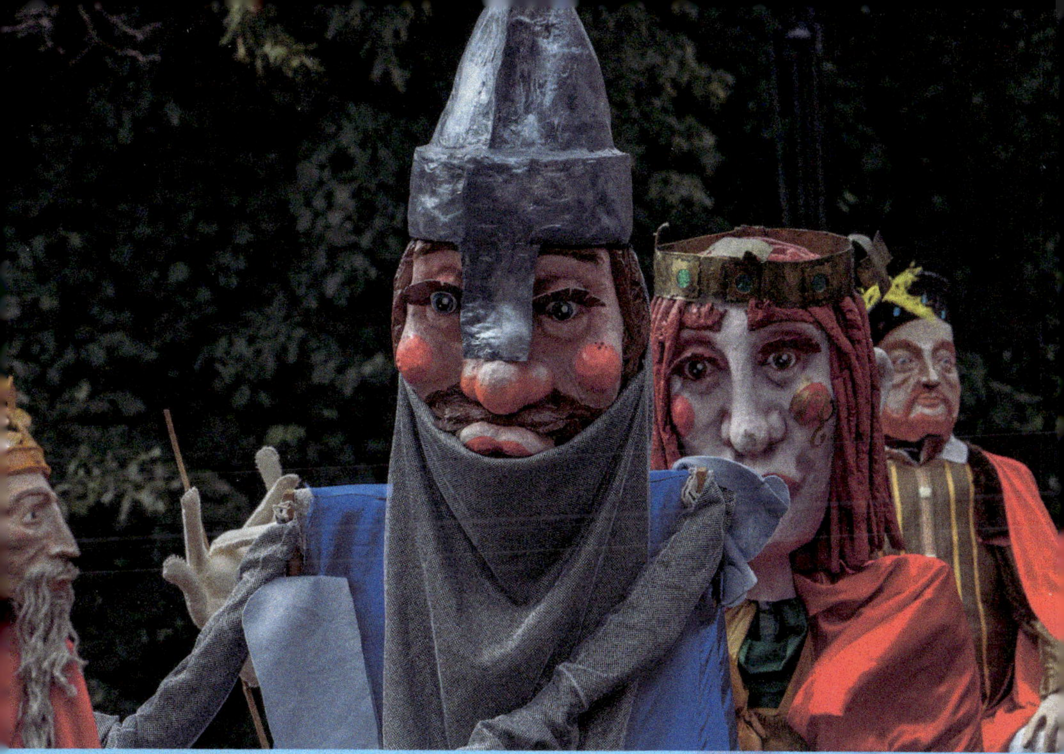

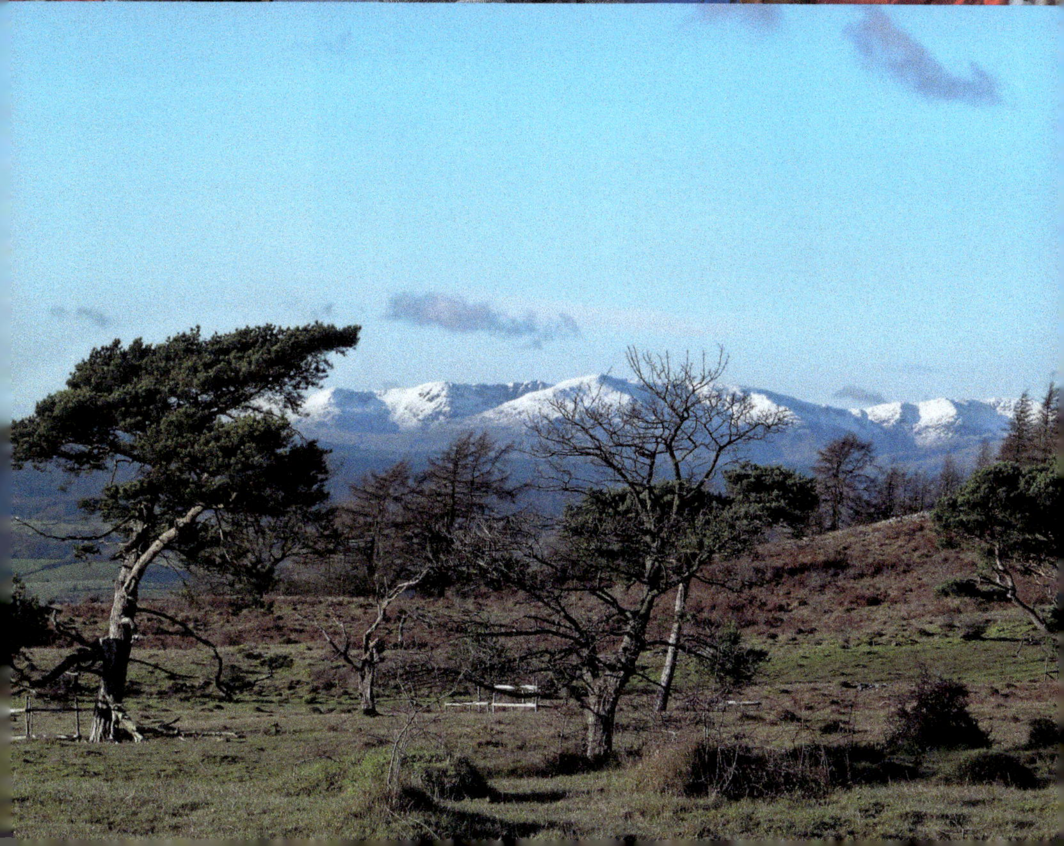

The coast and its estuaries can therefore make a good wet weather alternative to the Lake District fells as well as having their own attractions. With cooling sea breezes they can also be a good place to escape the crowds on a hot summer's day.

The warmest months are from April to October, which is the main tourist season. Some attractions only open seasonally so it is important to check websites before travelling.

Many festivals take place at this time. There is something for everyone, including traditional agricultural fairs, outdoor concerts, and mountain, literary and food festivals. Well-known examples within easy reach of the coast include the Ulverston and Silloth carnivals, the Egremont Crab Fair and the Cumbria Steam Gathering at Cark Airfield near Grange-over-Sands. To find more ideas, it is worth checking tourist information websites, and links are given later.

For walking enthusiasts, walking festivals are popular, typically featuring guided walks to local sights and fells. The Ulverston and Barrow-in-Furness walking festivals are good examples. The Lake District National Park Authority also organises an extensive programme of guided walks, some in coastal and estuary locations (www.lakedistrict.gov.uk).

Heritage Open Days in September are another great idea as they give the chance to visit places not normally open to the public (www.heritageopendays.org.uk). Examples in recent years have included tours of the tower at Carlisle Cathedral and walks with an expert guide across the sands from Walney Island to Piel Island.

During winter, most major towns have Christmas fairs. More unusual events include the Light Up Lancaster festival, the City of Lights festival in Carlisle, and Ulverston's Lantern and Dickensian Christmas festivals. More generally, the crisp clear air of a fine winter's day gives great views toward distant snow-covered peaks and winter is the best time to see migrating waterbirds, which gather in large numbers at some nature reserves.

Tourist information

In the area covered by this guide there are several tourist offices that can help with ideas for places to visit, finding accommodation and transport, and booking guided tours.

Two of the largest are in the two cities mentioned in this guide, in the main square in Carlisle and close to the railway station in Lancaster.

Further inland, other tourist offices include those operated by the Lake District National Park Authority in the market square in Keswick, in Bowness-on-Windermere, at the main visitor car park in Glenridding, and at Brockhole on Windermere, a stately home on the shores of the lake. Other large tourist offices include those in Morecambe and Dumfries.

More generally, information leaflets are widely available at tourist destinations and in railway, bus and motorway service stations. Much can also be found from an online search and some excellent sites for tourist information are:

▲ Tourist information office in Carlisle

- Visit Lake District
  (www.visitlakedistrict.com)
- Visit Cumbria (www.visitcumbria.com)
- Visit Lancashire
  (www.visitlancashire.com)
- Visit Scotland (www.visitscotland.com)

Many local authorities have visitor information on their websites and these are usually easy to find from an online search by typing the words 'visit' or 'discover' and a place name. Good examples include those for Grange-over-Sands, Ulverston, Barrow-in-Furness, Allerdale Council, and Allonby. Other great sources of information include the following regional sites:

- Explore Morecambe Bay
  (www.exploremorecambebay.org.uk)
- Cumbrian coastal railway
  (www.communityrailcumbria.co.uk)
- Western Lake District & Coast
  (www.westernlakedistrict.com)
- Arnside and Silverdale AONB
  (www.arnsidesilverdaleaonb.org.uk)
- Solway Coast AONB
  (www.solwaycoastaonb.org.uk)

The two AONB websites also contain many insights into local history and wildlife.

Getting around

One of the best ways to visit the coast of Cumbria is by using the coastal railway that runs from Lancaster to Maryport, before heading inland to Carlisle. This consists of the Furness Line from Lancaster to Barrow-in-Furness and the Cumbrian Coast Line beyond.

Some trains are direct but others may require a change in Barrow or Maryport. Both Lancaster and Carlisle lie on the west coast mainline with connections to Scotland and London.

The coastal railway is popular with both commuters and tourists and some

16 | THE CUMBRIA AND LAKE DISTRICT COAST

▲ Coastal views from Maryport Harbour

▲ Saltmarsh along the Solway Firth near Drumburgh

▲ Carnforth Station near Lancaster, where a museum celebrates filming of the 1940s classic Brief Encounter

sections are extremely scenic, particularly when crossing the viaducts across the Kent, Leven and Duddon estuaries. Of the places mentioned in this guide, those with stations nearby include Carnforth, Silverdale, Arnside, Grange-over-Sands, Cark-in-Cartmel, Ulverston, Barrow-in-Furness, Millom, Ravenglass, St Bees, Whitehaven, Workington and Maryport, plus Lancaster and Carlisle, of course.

Day tickets and Rover tickets provide a significant cost saving, and bicycles can be carried on some services, although check on train operator websites whether bookings are required before planning a trip.

Most locations are served by bus and the Cumbria County Council website contains links to the main operators (www.cumbria.gov.uk). Day and weekly passes are worth looking out for. On the Solway Firth there are bus services to the coast from Maryport, Wigtown and Carlisle, which all have rail stations for onward connections.

For both rail and bus transport, the national route planner service Traveline (www.traveline.info) is a useful source of information, as is the Visit Lake District website (www.visitlakedistrict.com).

Another option is to travel by car although this is increasingly discouraged due to congestion and for environmental reasons. If public transport isn't an option, electric cars are a partial solution and the Co-Wheels Car Club has pickup points at several major train stations (www.co-wheels.org.uk). The Lake District National Park website has a list of charging points (www.lakedistrict.gov.uk).

Guided tours are another possibility. Local companies include Mountain Goat Tours (www.mountain-goat.com) and Solway Connections, who run tours along the Solway Firth (www.solwayconnections.co.uk). Tourist information sites may suggest other possibilities.

Cycling around the coast

Cycling is one of the finest ways to explore an area and there are two cycleways along the coast.

In the south, the Bay Cycle Way follows cycle paths and minor roads from Glasson Dock near Lancaster to Barrow-in-Furness on the opposite side of Morecambe Bay (www.sustrans.org.uk). The route takes in many of the sights in this guide along the way.

Further north, there is a cycleway between Maryport and Silloth. The minor roads around the Cardurnock Peninsula west of Carlisle are also popular with cyclists, with great views out over the Solway Firth.

Elsewhere, coastal roads are sometimes busy, particularly between Barrow-in-Furness and Whitehaven. Here, the train is perhaps a better option, stopping off to explore the minor roads and lanes nearby.

A good starting point to find out more is to look on the websites of towns and councils in the area, which often have free-to-download cycling maps and guides.

More generally it is worth exploring the website of the Sustrans cycling charity, which has an excellent choice of routes and maps, as well as information on cycle safety and bike maintenance. Other topics include education, improving cycle safety, and the National Cycle Network. A variety of interesting blog posts and downloads are available, such as the useful video 'Check your bike is safe to ride'.

Long-distance walks and cycle routes

For hillwalkers and cyclists, a major attraction of Cumbria is the wide choice of long-distance walks and cycle routes.

One of the most popular walking routes is the Coast to Coast path. This begins in St Bees and crosses the Lake District, Yorkshire Dales and North York Moors to reach the North Sea

▼ The start of the C2C cycle route in Workington

▼ An England Coast Path sign in Silecroft

THE COASTAL VIEWPOINTS IN THIS GUIDE

One of the finest ways to see the coast is from on high and later chapters give suggestions for places to visit for a bird's eye view. Maps and guidebooks are available from most bookshops in the area with up-to-date route information, such as the maps produced by Ordnance Survey and Harvey Maps.

Although most walks are straightforward, all require suitable clothing and footwear and some a good level of fitness and hillwalking experience. Examples include Black Combe (600m) near the Duddon Estuary and Criffel (569m) overlooking the Solway Firth.

The weather is often changeable even in summer and a fine day can rapidly turn to mist, rain and even snow, so good navigation skills are required. Sensible precautions include taking a map, compass, mobile phone, torch, whistle and first aid kit, and spare batteries, food and clothing; also, an emergency shelter, such as the small bivvy bags found in most camping shops.

It is also important to check the mountain weather before setting off. Sources of hillwalking weather information include the Met Office's specialized Mountain Weather Forecast (www.metoffice.gov.uk) and the Mountain Weather Information Service (www.mwis.org.uk).

The Ramblers website is a great place to find out more about walking safely, both in the hills and on lowland and coastal paths (www.ramblers.org.uk). It also contains a wealth of information on getting fit, groups to join, navigation, and equipment to take.

▼ Near the summit of Black Combe (600m) on a winter's day

coast at Robin Hood's Bay near Whitby (www.coasttocoast.uk). The route was established by Alfred Wainwright who is famed for his pioneering walking guides and a set of peaks that feature in his books. In total there are 214 Wainwrights in the Lake District. Some of the viewpoints mentioned later appear in his book *The Outlying Fells of Lakeland*.

For cyclists, the counterpart to the Coast to Coast path is the C2C route, with a choice of starting in Whitehaven or Workington and ending near Sunderland or Tynemouth (www.sustrans.org.uk). The 'C' here stands for the word 'Sea' and in Workington the start is at the end of a pier at the mouth of the Derwent Estuary, where C2C is written in large letters on a port building. Another coast to coast route, the Reivers Route, starts in Whitehaven but heads further north through the Kielder Forest and Northumberland to Tynemouth.

For walkers, the Hadrian's Wall Path is a great long-distance walk that follows the route of the wall from Bowness-on-Solway to Wallsend near Newcastle (www.nationaltrail.co.uk). It begins at a raised walkway overlooking the Solway Firth, where information boards describe the route and local history and wildlife.

The wall is a UNESCO World Heritage Site and highlights along the way include museums and the ruins of spectacular hill forts. Some walkers choose to do the route in Roman headgear and clothing, which is an unusual spectacle for visitors to the Solway shores! As an alternative, Hadrian's Cycleway starts in Ravenglass and ends in South Shields (www.sustrans.org.uk).

▲ When visiting the countryside, it is important to consider the provisions of the Countryside Code regarding respect for other people, protecting the natural environment and enjoying the outdoors. This bookmark gives a brief summary and the full version is available from www.gov.uk (contains public sector information licensed under the Open Government Licence v3.0)

Other long-distance walks and cycle routes that begin at or near the coast include the Bay Cycle Way (see earlier) and the following routes:

- Walney-to-Wear: a cycle route from Walney Island with a choice of

finishing in Whitby or Sunderland (www.cyclingw2w.info)
- The Cumbria Way: a walk across the Lake District from Ulverston to Carlisle (www.cumbriawaywalk.info)

Until about a decade ago, there was a walking route around the coast of Cumbria, called the Cumbria Coastal Way. This stretched for about 180 miles, but is no longer supported.

However, the England Coast Path will soon become an alternative, and when complete will cover the whole coastline of England. It will be the longest coastal trail in the world, with a length of about 2,800 miles. The route is being opened in sections and in Cumbria already extends from Allonby to Silecroft and around Walney Island; see the National Trails website for the latest information (www.nationaltrail.co.uk).

▲ Bay Search & Rescue airboat (top) and Sherp (bottom)

Water safety

The Cumbrian coastline is hugely varied, with rugged sandstone cliffs, mudflats and wide sandy beaches, but one constant theme is the high tidal range. In estuaries, the funnelling effect from the shoreline adds to the risk, creating powerful currents that can easily catch people out.

Add in areas of soft mud and quicksand, and it is not surprising that there are many rescues on these shores, even of people trapped just a few metres from dry land.

The task of rescuing people falls to the RNLI (www.rnli.org) and other independent volunteer inshore rescue groups around the coast, with helicopter support from the Maritime & Coastguard Agency.

Most lifeboat stations operate fast, manoeuvrable RIBs (rigid inflatable boats) and some RNLI stations such as at Fleetwood, Barrow-in-Furness and Workington have larger all-weather craft.

Around Morecambe Bay, some stations have more specialized equipment for rescues from the sands, such as a hovercraft operated by the RNLI from Morecambe lifeboat station.

Bay Search & Rescue in Flookburgh (www.baysearchandrescue.org.uk) also have several all-terrain vehicles and an airboat similar to those seen skimming across the Florida Everglades in the movies. The latest addition is a futuristic-looking amphibious all-terrain vehicle called a Sherp, with outsize wheels and an enclosed cabin. The wheels can be inflated and deflated as required and act as paddles when it is afloat. The service is increasingly called upon to help with flood and snow rescues too.

Quicksand is formed from a mixture of sand and clay and becomes more mobile when pressure is applied, such as the weight of a person. As they struggle to escape, it becomes more solid, trapping the victim. Essential rescue equipment includes high-pressure jets to blast away material and inflatable rescue paths to spread a rescuer's weight across the surface. Due to the incoming tide, the time pressure during these types of rescue can be immense. The following section reproduces some excellent safety advice from the RNLI on the risks from the tides. Their website contains a wealth of information on other risks, such as riptides, waves and quicksand.

As charities, the RNLI and other independent rescue services rely on donations. Ways to support them include becoming a member, helping with fundraising, and using the gift shops at lifeboat stations. There are also charity shops, such as those run by Bay Search & Rescue in Milnthorpe and Grange-over-Sands. Many hold annual open days which make a great day out and give the chance for a close-up view of the lifeboats and rescue equipment.

▼ Road flooded at high tide near Lancaster and a warning sign in Arnside

Tidal cut-off

Swimming and other water sports aren't the only ways that people get into trouble at the beach. Getting cut off by the tide also contributes to a significant number of RNLI rescues every year.

Because tide times and heights vary throughout the month, a beach that was clear yesterday at 5pm might be completely covered in sea at the same time today.

Tides have a reputation for being unpredictable, but really they follow a timetable more reliable than most trains! There are two different types: spring and neap.

Spring tides have greater depth range between high and low water, so at high tide the water comes in further up the beach.

Neap tides have less variation, so at high tide the water won't come in as far.

Check the tide conditions and your surroundings

The UK and Ireland have some of the biggest tidal ranges in the world.

To avoid getting cut off by the tide:

- Before you head out, make sure it's safe. Check the tide tables.
- While you're out, be aware of your surroundings and the tide's direction.

A beach can seem like a vast playground but the tide can come in surprisingly quickly.

As the tide moves up and down the beach, the depth of the water changes throughout the day, sometimes by as much as 10 metres.

As the tide comes in, simply walking further up the beach and away to safety might not be an option.

If you've walked round to another cove at low tide, or walked around an outcrop of rocks, the water can soon block your way back as the tide turns. If the cove you're in doesn't have steps or access of its own, you could be in trouble.

Don't get cut off by the tide, check them

You can find out more information about tides in your area through tide tables, apps, weather news or local websites.

You can also get local tidal information from the Harbour Master, tourist information centre and some seaside retail outlets.

- Check forecasts and tides at RNLI lifeguarded beaches.
- Or find tide tables and surf reports for the UK and Ireland at magicseaweed.com.

Reproduced from the RNLI website (www.rnli.org/safety)

Webpage for donations: https://rnli.org/support-us/give-money

(Top) An RNLI hovercraft at Morecambe lifeboat station ▶

(Bottom) RNLI Barrow's Grace Dixon lifeboat passing Piel Castle at an open day in 2017 ▶

Morecambe lifeboat station
Lifeboats
RNLI
MAN
Lifeboats
HT-03
HF11 DXZ

Lifeboats

Kent Estuary near Sandside at sunset

chapter 1

COASTAL THEMES

The Lake District and Cumbrian coastline is highly varied with holiday resorts, estuaries, industrial towns, nature reserves and remote beaches. The habitat around its shores includes saltmarsh, sand dunes and lowland raised mires, which are all increasingly rare.

Signs of historic coastal settlement include stone circles and the remains of Roman coastal defences. In medieval times the area's historic abbeys and priories had an active coastal trade, although it was during the industrial revolution that most ports were established.

The large tidal range makes navigation challenging and tidal bores sometimes form on the highest tides. At low tide vast areas of mudflats and sandbanks are exposed and in winter these attract waterbirds, such as dunlins, curlews and oystercatchers. Other migratory species include ospreys, salmon, sea trout and eels.

THE CUMBRIA AND LAKE DISTRICT COAST

Habitat

Many of the landforms we see in Cumbria can be traced back to the end of the last Ice Age, more than ten thousand years ago.

Much of the area was covered by ice sheets. An ice dome covered the central Lake District from which glaciers spread out, carving valleys like spokes on a wheel. Further north, the flow turned west on meeting ice from the Scottish mountains.

As the glaciers melted, lakes formed in the rock basins left behind, feeding rivers that fanned out to the coast. As sea levels rose, some low-lying valleys became estuaries, with rivers and the ebb and flow of the tides depositing sand and silt to create mudflats and sandbanks.

In some places, peat bogs formed along the coastal margins and sand dunes at estuary mouths. Saltmarsh formed in areas inundated by the tide, with salt-tolerant plants such as samphire, glasswort, scurvy grass and thrift providing rich feeding grounds for insects and birds. Further inland, much of the Lake District was forested with oak, alder and other native broadleaf species.

The impact of coastal settlement is superimposed on this landscape and began a surprisingly long time ago. The first large-scale tree clearances occurred over five thousand years ago and continued during the Roman occupation

Borrowdale near Keswick has some of the most extensive broadleaf forest cover in the Lake District ▼

from the first century AD. From about a thousand years ago sheep farming hastened the loss of natural habitat. These changes were accelerated in medieval times as land was cleared for agriculture by monastic and aristocratic landowners.

In the 19th century, industrial-scale excavation led to loss of much of the peatlands, and in recent decades land management practices have threatened the habitat of sand dunes. Conifer plantations became increasingly widespread after World War 2, replacing native species.

In recent decades there has been a major effort to protect and restore areas at risk, including coastal habitats such as peatland, saltmarsh and sand dunes. Later sections give examples of the work performed by organisations such as Natural England, Cumbria Wildlife Trust and the RSPB. Another significant development is the expansion of broadleaf woodland as a way of controlling the pollution into lakes used for water supply.

Lowland raised mires

In Cumbria, lowland raised mires or peat bogs are a remarkable habitat found along the coastal plains of the Solway Firth, Morecambe Bay and the Duddon Estuary. They are formed from the remains of a plant called sphagnum moss which thrived in the many marshes and ponds that developed in the rock-scoured hollows left when the ice melted after the last Ice Age.

There are several species of this moss, in a rich variety of colours, but all with leaves capable of absorbing huge quantities of water. As plants decayed the layers below were compressed to

▲ Striding Edge on Helvellyn (950m), one of the most famous ridges in the Lake District

▲ Ulverston viewed across saltmarsh from near Sand Gate on the Leven Estuary

ENVIRONMENTAL PROTECTION

Due to their unique habitat, wildlife and geology, many estuary and coastal areas around Cumbria have some form of environmental protection and the following table summarises the most common types.

TYPE	ABBREV.	PURPOSE	EXAMPLE
Site of Special Scientific Interest	SSSI	National designation for habitat and wildlife	Arnside Knott SSSI
Special Protection Area	SPA	European directive for bird species	Morecambe Bay & Duddon Estuary SPA
Special Area of Conservation	SAC	European directive for habitat	Drigg Coast SAC
Ramsar	-	Wetlands of international importance	Morecambe Bay Ramsar
Local Nature Reserve	LNR	Local authority designation	Millom Ironworks LNR
National Nature Reserve	NNR	National designation	Roudsea Wood and Mosses NNR
National Park	NP	National designation	Lake District National Park
Area of Outstanding Natural Beauty	AONB	Natural England designation	Solway Coast AONB
Marine Conservation Zone	MCZ	Marine protected areas in coastal waters	Solway Firth MCZ

The main differences relate to the size of an area and its habitat and species. For example, a Special Protection Area (SPA) is specifically for birds, while an Area of Outstanding Natural Beauty (AONB), although smaller, shares many of the characteristics of a National Park. Areas can also overlap; for example, there are several Sites of Special Scientific Interest (SSSIs) within the Arnside and Silverdale AONB.

The environmental concerns addressed include pollution risks, coastal erosion, flooding, climate change, degradation of habitat and loss of species. Much progress has been made in recent decades and organisations working on these problems in Cumbria include:

- Government: Natural England, Environment Agency, local authorities, Forestry England
- Charities: National Trust, Cumbria Wildlife Trust, RSPB, Friends of the Lake District
- Rivers Trusts: South Cumbria, West Cumbria and Eden Rivers Trusts
- Others: community organisations, water companies (United Utilities)

Low tide on the Solway Firth ▼

form a dense organic material, peat. Depths can exceed ten metres, but this is a slow process and it takes about a thousand years to create each metre of peat. Typically, the surface forms a dome above the level of the surrounding land, and remarkably this pulses up and down with changes in the water content.

Locally these are known as 'mosses', such as Foulshaw Moss near Morecambe Bay and Glasson Moss alongside the Solway Firth. In medieval times, peat was used for domestic heating and cooking, but the mosses were managed in a sustainable way at village and manorial level. However, during the industrial revolution, extraction began on a much larger scale and continued until the middle of the 20th century. This also led to a drop in the water table, affecting the surrounding forests – known as wet woodland – often exacerbated by drainage for agriculture in nearby land.

Nowadays, lowland raised mires are recognised as a unique habitat that supports many rare types of birds, plants and insects. The multi-coloured mosses themselves are an attractive feature, and the carbon they absorb also helps to slow climate change. This has led to a global effort to restore the remaining areas and the techniques used to retain water include blocking drains, removing selected trees and scrub, and building small dams. Often this requires the use of excavators and other machinery.

In Cumbria, the RSPB, Natural England and Cumbria Wildlife Trust manage several reserves on lowland raised mires and these are described in later chapters. Visitor facilities typically include raised walkways to cross the restored bog and viewing platforms to better appreciate the scale and nature of the terrain. Wildlife species range from skylarks, dragonflies, butterflies and lizards, to fly-eating sundews, a rare example of a carnivorous species of plant.

▼ Lowland raised mire near the Solway Firth

Sand dunes

Sand dunes are found around the mouths of several estuaries in Cumbria and along the Irish Sea coast. They are valued for their unique habitat and offer some measure of flood protection to areas inland.

Coastal dune systems form when sand is deposited by the prevailing winds, initially accumulating around vegetation, rocks and other obstacles near the shoreline. They tend to form along the line of a beach, interspersed by valleys known as slacks. Further back from the shore, the more mature dunes can be many metres high.

In its natural state, a dune system is dynamic, with an ever-changing mix of open sand, sheltered slopes, ponds and vegetated areas. This provides a rich mosaic of habitat for amphibians, insects and birds, with many rare plant species. Indeed, the dunes in Cumbria are one of the last strongholds for the increasingly rare natterjack toad.

In recent decades, the usual approach to land management has been to stabilize dunes by allowing vegetation to grow, fencing them off to keep grazing animals away. This crowds out native plants, while invasive plant species, many imported in Victorian times, have added to the problem.

To help improve the situation, a project called Dynamic Dunescapes is considering nine locations around the UK, including the following dune systems in Cumbria:

- Morecambe Bay: North Walney, South Walney
- Duddon Estuary: Haverigg, Sandscale Haws
- Ravenglass Estuary: Eskmeals Dunes, Drigg Dunes
- Solway Firth: Grune Point, Mawbray Banks

Activities include clearing scrub and invasive species, introducing grazing animals, creating and fencing off ponds, and encouraging sand movement by creating gaps for the wind to blow through.

This involves working closely with local communities via schools and

Sand dunes near the mouth of the Ravenglass Estuary ▼

COASTAL THEMES | 31

volunteers to help rejuvenate the dunes. Contributions include long-term citizen science, community arts projects, school partnerships and public events. The project is being led by Natural England in collaboration with the Cumbria Wildlife Trust and the National Trust, and is funded by the National Lottery Heritage Fund and EU LIFE Programme (www.dynamicdunescapes.co.uk).

Rewilding

In conservation, a popular topic for debate is the scope for rewilding. Definitions vary but usually this means allowing nature to take its course and removing barriers to that happening. This should help wildlife to make a comeback, with selected species being reintroduced where appropriate.

In the UK, one of the largest rewilding projects is Wild Ennerdale in west Cumbria. Established in 2002, it is situated in the Ennerdale Valley, which is popular with outdoor enthusiasts and nature lovers. Ennerdale Water, one of the most scenic lakes in the Lake District, is the source of the River Ehen, which flows down to the Irish Sea. The project is a partnership between

(Top Right) The River Liza;
(Bottom Left) The upper Ennerdale Valley;
(Bottom Right) Black Galloway cattle near Ennerdale Water ▼▶

Forestry England, Natural England, the National Trust and United Utilities (www.wildennerdale.co.uk).

Archaeological studies suggest that Ennerdale has been inhabited for several thousand years. Originally the valley was largely forested but tree clearance began in the Bronze Age, with sheep introduced about a thousand years ago. Mining for iron ore began in medieval times and continued into the 19th century. In the lower parts of the valley cattle were reared in the middle ages and deer still remain, descendants from a deer park established in those times. In common with many other Lake District valleys, large-scale conifer planting began in the past hundred years.

Since the project began, conifer plantations have been increasingly replaced with native broadleaf species. Embankments have also been removed to allow the river that flows into Ennerdale Water – the Liza – to follow a more natural course. Due to storms, it has already made some dramatic excursions across the valley floor, felling trees and creating new habitat, such as woody debris dams, gravel beds and ponds.

Black Galloway cattle have also been introduced into the valley. These are a hardy species whose grazing patterns are similar to those of now extinct species such as the auroch, a type of wild cow, and the European bison. This has allowed native tree and flower seedlings to thrive. Wildlife species that are making a return include red squirrels, otters, the marsh fritillary butterfly and, in Ennerdale Water, the rare arctic char, a cold-water fish related to salmon and trout.

Maritime History

Early history

Some of the earliest settlers in Cumbria were in the coastal region. The coastal waters provided rich fishing grounds, with a milder climate than in nearby mountain areas.

The earliest human remains to be discovered were found in a cave near the Kent Estuary and date from about ten thousand years ago. Exhibits from the site at the Dock Museum in Barrow-in-Furness include a fragment of human leg bone and a lynx jaw bone. Stone tools from even earlier times, about twelve

Stone circle at Birkrigg Common near Ulverston ▼

Holme Cultram Abbey near Silloth ▼

HADRIAN'S WALL

Hadrian's Wall was built some seventy years after the Roman Conquest to defend the northern boundary of the Roman Empire. The wall was named after Hadrian, the emperor in charge of forces at that time.

Construction began in AD 122 and the wall stretched from Bowness-on-Solway to Wallsend to the east of Newcastle. Along the Solway Firth, a key role was to prevent attack at low tide by invaders crossing the sands, and it incorporated existing defences at crossing points near Bowness-on-Solway, Drumburgh and Burgh by Sands.

Further along the coast, a risk still remained from the sea, so the defensive line was continued but in a smaller way. This used a similar pattern of forts interspersed with smaller forts called milefortlets and watchtowers or turrets, but with no wall between them. As the name suggests, milefortlets were spaced at intervals of a Roman mile, which is slightly shorter than its modern equivalent.

The southernmost extent was about a mile beyond Maryport, which was probably chosen as it would require a long sea crossing to reach this point, much reducing the risk of attack. The only known defences further along the coast were isolated coastal forts at Ravenglass and at Burrow Walls near Workington and Moresby near Whitehaven. The fort at Ravenglass was built to protect the natural harbour there. This was an important supply route along a Roman road that led to inland forts at Hardknott and Ambleside.

The defences incorporated existing forts at Maryport and Carlisle. The main supply route was via Maryport. The fort here was on cliffs overlooking a harbour and the Senhouse Roman Museum lies next to the excavated remains (www.senhousemuseum.co.uk). Many of the artefacts found are on display at the museum, along with finds from a larger civilian settlement or *vicus* to the north, which included a temple. The types of ships used probably included Roman galleys powered by sail and two or more tiers of oars.

Other fascinating places to visit in Cumbria to learn more about the Roman coastal presence include:

- Ravenglass, where the remains of the bath house are some of the best preserved in the UK
- Crosscanonby, where the first total excavation of a milefortlet can be seen (Milefortlet 21)
- Carlisle, where the Tullie House Museum & Art Gallery has an entire floor dedicated to Roman history (www.tulliehouse.co.uk)

These are described in later chapters. Further inland, the ruins of Hardknott and Ambleside forts may be of interest (www.english-heritage.org.uk) and there are of course many spectacular places to visit along Hadrian's Wall (www.hadrianswallcountry.co.uk).

(Left) Cavalry during a Roman re-enactment in Carlisle;
(Right) Ruins of a Roman bath house near Ravenglass ▼

thousand years ago, have been found elsewhere in south Cumbria.

Stone circles provide perhaps the clearest evidence of human settlement and there are about fifty sites across Cumbria. The most dramatic is at Castlerigg, near Keswick, which dates from about 3000 BC (www.english-heritage.org.uk). A circle of thirty-eight stones stands up to about three metres tall on a hill looking south along the Thirlmere Valley. This is a truly dramatic location, particularly when swirling mist and shafts of sunlight add to the atmosphere.

Around the coast, the best-preserved sites are at Birkrigg Common, overlooking the Leven Estuary, and Swinside, high above the Duddon Estuary. These are described in later chapters. Other examples near the coast include Grey Croft Stone Circle, near Seascale, and Kinniside Stone Circle, near Ennerdale.

The Roman occupation began in the first century AD and the Solway Firth formed part of the northern boundary. The Roman ports at Ravenglass and Maryport are described later. A succession of invaders then settled in the area, including the Vikings, and the Dock Museum in Barrow-in-Furness and the Beacon Museum in Whitehaven have many reminders of their presence.

After the Norman Conquest, monastic orders controlled large tracts of land, raising sheep and cattle, growing crops and importing and exporting goods via the coast. In the south, Cartmel Priory traded via Grange-over-Sands, while Piel Castle near Walney Island was a defensive outpost and fortified store for nearby Furness Abbey. St Bees Priory controlled much of western Cumbria, trading via Whitehaven. Further north, Holme Cultram Abbey oversaw lands along the coast of the Solway Firth, with a beach port at Skinburness, later moved to Newton Arlosh.

The products traded included grain, leather, wool, timber, charcoal and salt. In south Cumbria, goods such as barrels and combs were produced from the extensive woodlands, which were managed using a traditional sustainable approach called coppicing.

This period also marked the start of the iron and coal industries. For example, Furness Abbey derived much of its wealth from iron smelting, using small charcoal-fired furnaces called bloomeries; further north, coal mining began under the control of St Bees Priory.

On a smaller scale, fortified churches and farms dotted the land, including the distinctive square shaped pele towers that provided villagers with a place of refuge during an attack. To the north, one threat came from the border reivers, who were notorious for cattle and sheep rustling, smuggling and other nefarious activities.

Industrial Revolution

As coastal trade increased, estuaries provided a convenient way to move goods inland for onward transport by mule or horse and cart. Settlements with quays and wharves included Old Sandsfield on the Solway Firth, west of Carlisle, and Milnthorpe on the River Bela in the Kent Estuary, which was an important port for Kendal.

Other busy ports around Morecambe Bay included Greenodd on the Leven

Estuary, near to Ulverston, and Skippool Creek, upstream from Fleetwood, which was once one of the largest ports in the region.

As the industrial revolution got underway, ship sizes increased, prompting a need for deep water ports, and this spurred the growth of towns such as Barrow-in-Furness, whose roots are described later. The Ulverston, Carlisle and Lancaster canals were built to provide links to the coast.

The Lancaster Canal was the longest and by 1826 provided a route between Lancaster, Kendal, Preston and the coast at Glasson Dock. At the other extreme, the Ulverston Canal was less than two miles long and was built to provide the town with a link to the Leven Estuary. The Carlisle Canal played a similar role, connecting Carlisle to a new port, Port Carlisle, on the shores of the Solway Firth.

From the mid-19th century, steamships allowed coastal transport to become faster and more reliable, as they were less affected by the vagaries of the wind than sailing ships. At the height of coastal activity, scheduled services included those to Liverpool from Greenodd, Lancaster, Whitehaven and Port Carlisle, and the Isle of Man from Whitehaven and Greenodd. Pleasure steamers also operated from Fleetwood to Roa Island near Barrow,

(Top to bottom) Greenside Mine near Ullswater in the Lake District, which produced lead and silver from 1825 to 1961; Remains of lock gates on the Ulverston Canal; The restored Stott Park Bobbin Mill near Windermere (www.english-heritage.org.uk). Bobbins were spindles used in spinning and weaving and were mass-produced for the mills of Lancashire ▶

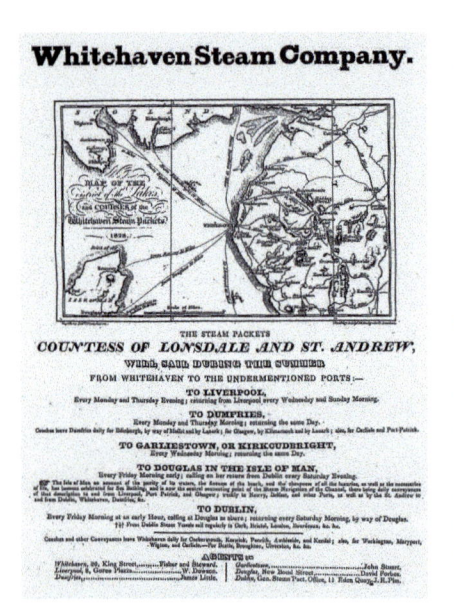

▲ A Whitehaven Steam Packet poster; the title reads 'Map of the district of the Lakes and courses of the Whitehaven steam packets 1828' (credit: CRC/Beacon Museum)

with onward connections to Windermere for visitors to the Lake District.

This period also saw the introduction of the railways and this marked the start of a reduction in coastal trade. This was later accelerated by the decline in the coal mining and iron ore industries. Few signs now remain of the Carlisle Canal although the Lancaster Canal is popular for leisure boating and the towpath of the Ulverston Canal provides a scenic way to reach the shores of the Leven Estuary from the town.

Nowadays the railway network is also much diminished, in particular since the Beeching cuts in the 1960s. Lines that have been closed since then include the Cockermouth, Keswick and Penrith Railway, which connected with trains to Workington, and the Carlisle and Silloth Bay Railway. Another closure, earlier in the century, was a route north to Scotland via Annan. This travelled over a dramatic viaduct over the Solway Firth, whose remains are still visible near Bowness-on-Solway.

Shipping, geology and mining

During the industrial revolution, much coastal trade revolved around locally extracted products such as slate, coal and iron ore. Several of the ports and harbours around the coastline were originally established to serve these industries. Goods traded in return included tobacco, sugar, raw cotton and Baltic timber.

Between Barrow and the Solway Firth, most of the coastal plain is underlain by red sandstone dating from the Permian and Triassic periods, more than two hundred million years ago. Although mostly hidden by glacial boulder-clay deposits, this can be seen dramatically at the cliffs at St Bees, the only significant cliffs in northwest England.

From Whitehaven to Maryport there is a band of carboniferous limestone rich in coal seams, which extends east around the northern part of the Lake District. Coal mining became an important activity, leading to the growth of these two ports and of the nearby towns of Harrington and Workington. Deep coal mines extended out beneath the sea, making for a dangerous working environment.

Inland, Skiddaw Slates dominate the northern Lake District, while the central area is underlain by the hard lavas of the Borrowdale Volcanic Group, whose resistance to erosion leads to some of the most dramatic peaks. Slates and shales then reappear around Windermere and the Coniston fells.

Further south, around Morecambe Bay, carboniferous limestone reappears, sometimes containing rich deposits of haematite from which iron can be smelted. This led to the growth of Barrow-in-Furness and Millom as ports for the export of iron ore and products. The limestone geology is most evident in the dramatic promontory of Humphrey Head on the Kent Estuary and the cliffs of nearby Whitbarrow Scar. Chapel Island in the Leven Estuary is another outcrop of limestone that escaped being ground down by the glaciers.

Other interesting geological features include an area of sandstone along the southern end of the Cartmel and Furness peninsulas, and an area of Skiddaw slate that is exposed in places at Black Combe (600m), which overlooks the Duddon Estuary. The islands at the extreme end of the Furness Peninsula were formed from glacial deposits, and evidence of this includes the many boulders and rocks whose geology is characteristic of areas further north.

In Cumbria, slate is still mined in places, including at Honister Slate Mine, which is now a popular tourist destination (www.honister.com). Iron ore mining ended at Millom in the 1960s and the last coal mine to be closed was Haig Colliery near Whitehaven in the 1980s.

(Top) Sandstone cliffs of St Bees Head ▶
(Bottom) Limestone outcrops of Whitbarrow Scar ▶

Later chapters describe several great places to learn more about the geology and mining history of Cumbria, including the Dock Museum in Barrow-in-Furness, Millom Heritage & Arts Centre, the Beacon Museum in Whitehaven, Maryport Maritime Museum and the Tullie House Museum & Art Gallery in Carlisle. Threlkeld Quarry & Mining Museum near Keswick is another fascinating place to visit (www.threlkeldquarryandminingmuseum.co.uk).

Modern-day operations

Nowadays the main commercial ports in Cumbria are at Barrow-in-Furness and Workington. These are also used by high-speed craft that service the many offshore windfarms that have sprung up along the coastline in recent decades. Further south, Fleetwood, Heysham and Glasson

▲ Southerness Lighthouse on the Solway Firth near Dumfries was built in the 18th century and used until the 1930s

A fishing boat returns to Maryport Harbour ▲

Dock are busy ports on the Lancashire shores of Morecambe Bay, and Fleetwood has a fishing fleet.

On the Solway Firth, the commercial port at Silloth is also home to a fishing fleet, as are the harbours at Whitehaven and Maryport. On the Scottish shores, Kirkcudbright is a major fishing port and Cairnryan, near Stranraer, just outside the Solway, is a busy departure point for Irish Sea ferries.

When navigating around these shores, it is important to be aware of the high tidal range, particularly if venturing into the estuaries. At low tide the key risk is from grounding on the sandbanks and mudflats. In the 18th century, it was routine to beach ships on the shores, propping them up with supports for loading and unloading. When the tide is rising or falling, the funnelling effect in estuaries causes strong currents, which are an additional challenge.

To safely navigate these waters, most large vessels must use the local pilotage service, whose pilots are expert mariners, able to guide ships in and out of port. For example, the port authorities at Barrow and Workington operate tugs to help with operations; the latter also providing pilot services to guide ships up the coast to Silloth.

Before the days of radio and then GPS, lighthouses were key navigation aids. These included Plover Scar Lighthouse near Lancaster, Walney Lighthouse at the southern tip of Walney Island, Hodbarrow Lighthouse near Millom, and a pair of lighthouses at both Fleetwood and Whitehaven. Smaller wooden towers out to sea, known as perches, were another common sight.

Leading light solutions were often used, requiring navigators to wait for lights to line up before making a turn. For example, in the Lune Estuary a second light was operated near Cockersand Abbey on the shore in conjunction with the Plover Scar Lighthouse out to sea.

FINDING OUT TIDE TIMES

Tidal predictions are essential for shipping operators, port authorities and leisure activities such as sailing, angling and coastal walks.

Despite the number of factors that affect the tides, they can be estimated with reasonable precision for weeks to months ahead. In the UK, the two main sources for predictions are the National Tidal and Sea Level Facility in Liverpool (www.ntslf.org) and the UK Admiralty Office in Southampton (www.admiralty.co.uk).

The weather section of the BBC website is another useful source (www.bbc.co.uk) and includes estimated values for a wide choice of locations.

Small booklets of tide tables are widely available in coastal areas. Good places to look include local newsagents, fishing tackle shops, and RNLI shops, such as those in Morecambe and Silloth. Printouts are sometimes placed on information boards at harbours. To help to estimate tide times at places not listed, booklets usually include correction factors for popular locations.

▲ Winter views of the Leven Estuary at high tide (left) and just over half an hour later (right)

Whatever the approach used, it is essential to check whether times are given in local time or Greenwich Mean Time (GMT). Tidal predictions are often in GMT, even after the clocks go forward in late March to British Summer Time. The difference is then plus one hour until the clocks go back in late October.

Astronomical tide predictions are often remarkably accurate. However, a phenomenon called surge can lead to large differences between observations and predictions and peak levels earlier than expected. Surge is a short-lived rise in water levels that typically occurs when there are storms in the Atlantic Ocean and Irish Sea. It occurs due to the action of the wind and, to a lesser extent, the decrease in atmospheric pressure.

The additional rise in sea levels can exceed 1-2 metres and lead to coastal flooding if it coincides with a high tide. When visiting the coast in these conditions, it is therefore particularly important to check if any flood warnings or alerts have been issued for coastal regions by the Environment Agency; search for the term 'flood warnings' on the Government website www.gov.uk.

This text is adapted from *The Mersey Estuary: A Travel Guide* by Kevin Sene

TIDAL BORES

In several of the estuaries around Cumbria, a most unusual sight occurs on the highest tides, that of a line of surf travelling upstream against the river flow. This is a tidal bore and it happens when the rate of rise of sea levels is so fast that a wave forms, breaking and reforming as it goes. Often this is followed by a series of smaller waves, called whelps.

Tidal bores occur in most of the estuaries around Morecambe Bay, in the Duddon Estuary, and in several estuaries around the Solway Firth. As with any natural phenomenon, predicting when they will occur is not an exact science, but contributing factors include:

- An unusually high spring tide
- Low river flows, such as after a dry spell
- Little or no wave action, such as when winds are light

Normally, when the tide comes in, the river flow seems to slow, becoming slack for a while, before changing direction. The power of the tide then gets established and can be a very impressive sight.

When a tidal bore forms, it is preceded by a wave and often a line of surf. In calm weather it is sometimes possible to hear the tide arriving as a whoosh of water in the distance, and glassy smooth water makes it easier to see. The sound of waterbirds startled into flight is often another cue.

Due to their unpredictability, it is best to arrive well in advance of the expected time for a tidal bore to pass. Be ready for disappointment, as it may take several visits before success. Usually it is easy to check if you have arrived in time, since the river flow will still be moving gently downstream toward the coast. However, if unsure, watch rocks and other objects on the shoreline, as they will rapidly become covered with water once the tide arrives.

The best viewing times are around the equinoxes, when spring tides are highest, and for a day or two either side. To predict whether a tidal bore is likely, the key information required is the predicted water level at high tide for a nearby site and the time when it will occur. A timing correction must then be applied, both for time it takes the tide to reach your chosen viewing location, and because tidal bores occur as the tide is rising, not at high tide. The table opposite gives **approximate** values for the tidal bores mentioned in this guide and later chapters give more details.

▼ The Arnside Bore in the Kent Estuary

When watching a tidal bore, it is important to pick a safe viewing location well above the predicted high water mark, as water levels will rise quickly once the bore has passed, sometimes by several metres in an hour. In particular, never venture out onto sandbanks, mudflats or saltmarsh as these will soon become covered in fast-flowing water. If travelling by car, another consideration is that parking areas can become flooded.

On the day, it is important to check if any flood warnings or alerts are in force before deciding whether to travel (www.gov.uk). The introduction to this guide gives more information on water safety.

LOCATION	ESTUARY	POSSIBLE VIEWPOINTS	TIDE MONITORING LOCATION	INDICATIVE MINIMUM HIGH TIDE LEVEL REQUIRED (METRES)	INDICATIVE TIME BEFORE HIGH TIDE THAT THE TIDAL BORE ARRIVES (HOURS)
Morecambe Bay	Wyre	Wardley Creek	Fleetwood	–	2–3
	Lune	Sunderland Point	Morecambe	–	3–4
		St George's Quay		–	1–2
	Kent	Arnside Pier	Barrow	9.5–10.0	1.5–2
	Leven	Canal Foot	Barrow	9.5	2–3
Irish Sea Solway Firth	Duddon	Dunnerholme	Barrow	–	–
	Eden	Bowness-on-Solway	Hestan Island	8.4–8.5	2–3
		Drumburgh			1–2
	Wampool	Angerton road bridge	Silloth	–	Around high tide
	Esk	Between Annan and Gretna	–	–	1–2
	Nith	Glencaple	Hestan Island	8.6	About 2
		Kingholm Quay			1–1.5
	Bladnoch	Near Wigtown	–	–	–

Viewing tips and sightseeing ideas

TIDAL BORES OF ENGLAND, SCOTLAND AND WALES

This information is adapted from the book 'Tidal Bores in England, Scotland and Wales' by Kevin Sene, which gives more background on why tidal bores occur and describes several others around the UK, including the Severn Bore.

SHIPPING AND THE TIDES

Shipping around Cumbria is strongly affected by the tides, which determine when ships can enter and leave port. Good piloting skills are required to cope with the strong currents that can occur, particularly in estuaries.

The tides occur due to the gravitational pull of the moon and, to a lesser extent, that of the sun, and are often called the astronomical tides. In most places around the world, water levels rise and fall on roughly a 12-hour cycle, with the time of the peaks advancing each day. That means that in the UK there are typically two peaks a day when water levels are at their highest.

The incoming tide is known as the flood tide, while the ebb tide occurs as water levels fall. The influences can extend far inland, such as on the River Wampool on the Solway Firth, where minor tidal flooding of roads and farmland can occur many miles from the coast.

Often the rise and fall is not symmetrical with the flood tide occurring faster than the ebb tide, such as near the top of the Solway Firth. Some factors that affect the timing include the depth of water near the shoreline and the shape of the coastline and sea bed. Many other forces are at play arising from variations in the orbits of the sun, moon and Earth.

Underlying this behaviour is a monthly cycle, so that every two weeks or so levels are unusually high. These are known as spring tides and the lowest levels in between are called neap tides. The meaning of the term 'spring' here is lost in the mists of time, but is not related to the season.

There is also an annual variation; tides are highest in spring and autumn, around the time of the equinoxes, when the clocks change to and from British Summer Time. This is often the best time to see tidal bores. It also offers an excellent opportunity to see wading birds which are forced closer to the shore by the rising tide.

This text is adapted from *The Mersey Estuary: A Travel Guide* by Kevin Sene

Available as an ebook from Troubador Publishing (www.troubador.co.uk) and most online retailers.

▼ Low tide on Morecambe Bay

Several of these lighthouses are still essential to navigation, although are now automated. These include the Plover Scar and Walney lighthouses, and the St Bees Lighthouse, which is situated high on the cliffs north of the town.

Wildlife

Marine life

The coastal waters of Morecambe Bay, the Irish Sea and the Solway Firth support a diverse range of marine life. These range from microscopic organisms to migratory fish such as salmon and marine mammals such as seals, dolphins and porpoises. Morecambe Bay in particular is famed for its cockles and mussels and the Solway Firth for prawn fishing.

Seals are perhaps the easiest mammals to spot as there is a resident population of several hundred at the Cumbria Wildlife Trust's South Walney Nature Reserve. These can sometimes be seen further afield, such as near the mouth of the Duddon Estuary.

Seals are occasionally spotted in the Solway Firth, although it seems likely that they are from colonies in Scotland or the Isle of Man. Perhaps the most dramatic sighting in recent years was of a seal pup about twenty miles inland on a tributary of the River Eden between Penrith and Appleby. This had probably chased fish inland and was rescued and returned to the sea by a team from Bay Search & Rescue, who are based at Flookburgh near Morecambe Bay.

Dolphins and porpoises are more elusive but are some of the most

▲ Seal pup at the South Walney Nature Reserve (© The Cumbria Wildlife Trust)

▲ The skeleton of Driggsby the Whale at Tullie House Museum & Art Gallery

interesting creatures to see around the Cumbria coastline. The most common species are harbour porpoise, common dolphin and the larger bottlenose dolphin, which grows up to four metres long.

Perhaps the best chance of a sighting is on a Sea Watch Foundation training course (www.seawatchfoundation.org.uk) or other public event such as the National Whale and Dolphin Watch in the last week of July. Viewing locations in Cumbria include St Bees Head and Maryport, and although sightings don't occur on every visit, they are fairly regular. In addition to scanning the horizon with binoculars, these events can include an interesting presentation on each species.

The foundation is a national charity working to improve the conservation and protection of whales, dolphins and porpoises in British and Irish waters. They also have a very informative public recording app called *Sea Watcher* that can be downloaded for free from the main app stores. It has many pictures and videos to help aid watching and species identification.

Further afield, porpoise sightings are surprisingly common from the promenade at Silloth. Whales are seen along the coast too, but sightings are rare, and usually from boats rather than the shore. There have been several strandings in recent years, including of a fin whale that was found at Drigg near the Ravenglass Estuary. Given the name Driggsby the Whale, the twelve metre long skeleton is now on display in Tullie House Museum & Art Gallery in Carlisle.

Minke whales are occasionally seen and there have even been a few sightings of humpback whales. Other unusual sightings in the Irish Sea and Solway Firth have included leatherback turtles and the plankton-eating basking shark, which grows to about ten metres long.

Migratory Fish

Estuaries provide a route inland for migratory fish, which seek the clear, sheltered waters of the Lake District fells to spawn. The species found around Cumbria are salmon, sea trout, eels, and the eel-like sea lamprey.

Many return to the rivers where they were raised. In recent decades, the Environment Agency and Rivers Trusts have been modifying rivers to help this to occur; steps taken include adding bristle strips and fish passes at weirs and moveable flaps at tide gates. As the name suggests, bristle strips have flexible spikes and are designed to allow eels to wriggle their way upstream; one site where they have been installed is at the weir at the outlet of Windermere.

Atlantic salmon are perhaps the best-known visitors and fish are sometimes seen leaping over waterfalls and weirs on their way upstream, such as on the rivers Kent and Leven. The best time to visit is in late autumn and early winter, but it may take many visits before being lucky. Upstream from the Leven, some make their way through Windermere to rivers further upstream.

The life cycle of the salmon is well known but still remarkable. It starts when young fish cross the Atlantic to northeast Canada and western Greenland, where they grow to full size before returning to the same river to breed some years later. They are thought to achieve this feat of navigation by 'smell' or 'taste', guided by the chemical and biological composition of the waters that they left.

This unusual life cycle has evolved since the upland spawning grounds provide good feeding, habitat and shelter for the small fry and parr. The oceans then provide larger prey, allowing adult fish to reach sizes

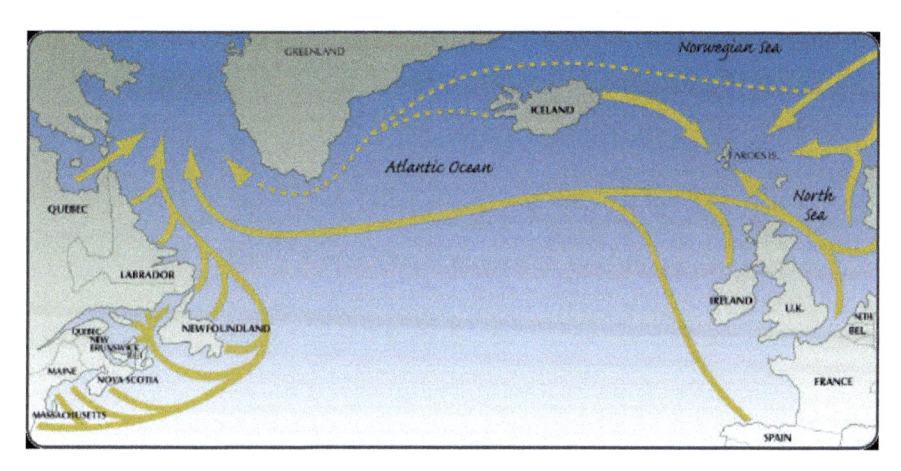

▲ Atlantic salmon travel thousands of miles to their North Atlantic feeding grounds (arrows), usually near western Greenland. They remain for one to three years before returning to their home river to reproduce (credit: U.S. Fish and Wildlife Service)

of a metre or more. However, less than a third survive to migrate again and only a small proportion return to spawn again. Salmon typically live for four to six years and in some cases up to ten years.

Eels are also found in the rivers of Cumbria and have a similarly dramatic life cycle. After hatching in the west Atlantic, eel larvae take one to three years to drift across to Europe, metamorphosing into transparent (glass) eels in the process. Then, as elvers, they gain their familiar black colour and move inland where they stay for several years before returning to their breeding grounds, now having gained a silver coloration.

At first sight, sea lamprey look like eels, but the adults have teeth and are parasitic, feeding by attaching themselves to larger fish. They are sometimes called the vampires of the deep. They typically spawn in the lower and middle reaches of rivers. The larvae then grow hidden in the river bed before metamorphosing into the adult form and migrating to the ocean. Sea lamprey are found in several rivers in Cumbria, including the Derwent, Eden and Leven, together with their freshwater cousins, the river and brook lamprey.

Like salmon, sea trout spawn in river waters. Spawning occurs during the autumn and winter months, with hatching the following spring. Then, aged one to three years, some adopt a silver appearance and migrate to the sea, but others remain in fresh water all their lives. The adult fish return up to three years later. Once back their colour changes again so that they look similar to brown trout, although thanks to the richer feeding grounds in the ocean, they are often considerably larger. Unlike salmon, some sea trout colonise different rivers on their return, and many migrate again after spawning, sometimes returning several times.

Waterbirds

Despite the fascinating marine life, the estuaries of Cumbria are best known for waterbirds. These feed on the mudflats exposed at low tide which are rich in prey such as shellfish, snails and worms. The shallow waters and creeks contain sand eels, crabs, mussels, cockles and prawns, all rich sources of protein.

In winter, about a quarter of a million wading birds, ducks and geese gather around Morecambe Bay, with many more on the Solway Firth and the Duddon Estuary. Common species include oystercatchers, redshanks, dunlins, knots, curlews, eider ducks and barnacle geese.

Most of these species are migratory, arriving in autumn and departing again in spring for destinations such as Canada, Siberia and the Arctic. For longer distance travellers the estuaries make a convenient refuelling stop on the way to southern Europe or West Africa. In contrast, some species arrive in spring to breed, such as little and common terns.

Wading birds are often seen feeding together as there is safety in numbers and they generally do not compete for food. For example, the curlew has a long, curving bill ideal for rooting out lugworms, snails and crabs, while turnstones feed at the surface looking for mussels and other prey with their short, strong beaks. Oystercatchers, despite their name, feed mainly on mussels and cockles.

Although on the ground some species appear drab, most are beautiful in flight, many with bold black, grey and white markings on long slender wings designed for long-distance travel. Satellite tracking by the Global Flyway Network has recorded a bar-tailed godwit travelling more than 7,500 miles across the Pacific from Alaska to New Zealand. This was done in a single flight taking just 11 days. Bar-tailed godwits are also found around the coast of Cumbria.

Another remarkable migration is that of barnacle geese, in which almost all the birds that nest on Svalbard in the Arctic spend winter on the Solway Firth. More than 40,000 birds gather in some years, forming spectacular flocks as they fly inland to feed in the morning and return to the Solway before dark. Caerlaverock Nature Reserve near Dumfries is an excellent place to see this behaviour.

The seabirds that nest on the cliffs at St Bees Head draw many wildlife enthusiasts. These are the only significant cliffs in northwest England and the species that gather here in spring include guillemots, fulmars and kittiwakes. Cormorants are also common and puffins are sighted occasionally. Further south, another spring visitor is the pair of ospreys that nest at Foulshaw Moss near the Kent Estuary and have raised chicks successfully for several years.

Ospreys

Ospreys are impressive fish-eating birds of prey, with a maximum wingspan of approximately 1.5 metres. They are one of the world's great travellers and the Eurasian species has a range which extends from Japan to West Africa and Scandinavia. Due to persecution, they became extinct in much of the UK during the 19th century although a few managed to survive in Scotland until the early 1900s. Breeding pairs then reappeared there in the 1950s and thanks to a major conservation effort there is now a breeding population of more than two hundred birds.

In the Lake District the 1830s marked the last sightings of nesting osprey although migrating birds continued to be seen occasionally, flying overhead or taking a break to fish or perch in tree tops. This encouraged enthusiasts from the Lake District National Park, the Forestry Commission and the RSPB to form the Lake District Osprey Project, based at Bassenthwaite Lake, near Keswick.

Since ospreys prefer flat nesting sites, one of the first steps was to build artificial platforms to attract a nesting pair, and the first successful hatching was in 2001, the year that the project began. Chicks are now raised successfully nearly every year. Visitors can watch the nest from a distant spot by telescope.

Once the eggs have been laid, the incubation period typically lasts for about a month. The chicks then take their first flights two months after hatching and are ready to migrate south a month later. Remarkably, the adults leave first, alone, not meeting again until the following spring, and the chicks follow later, finding their own way on their first migration. The young usually do not return for three years and choose a different site to that of their parents.

All new chicks are tagged for identification and – using GPS devices

▲ Guillemots at St Bees Head

– ospreys from the project have been tracked as far as the Sahara Desert, Ghana and the Ivory Coast, in one case reaching northern France in just a few hours. Normally the route across Spain to West Africa takes about two to three weeks.

This success spurred similar efforts to attract ospreys to south Cumbria at Cumbria Wildlife Trust's Foulshaw Moss Nature Reserve (www.cumbriawildlifetrust.org.uk). The reserve is part of a once extensive area of peat bog alongside the Kent Estuary and facilities

▼ Redshanks near Port Carlisle on the Solway Firth

▲ Barnacle geese at the RSPB Mersehead reserve on the Solway Firth

include raised walkways, a viewing platform and ponds that are havens for dragonflies and other insects.

Chicks have now been raised for several years and leg identification rings show that the pair are from Bassenthwaite and Kielder Water. The nesting platform is in a remote area of the reserve and the chances of seeing an osprey are greatly improved by going on one of the guided walks organised during the breeding season. The birds are often seen feeding in the Kent Estuary and further beyond, such as at the RSPB's Leighton Moss reserve.

The Birdwatchers' Code

Several leading bird organisations, magazines and websites have produced the following birdwatchers' code of conduct that puts the interests of birds first and respects other people, whether or not they are interested in birds. See the RSPB website for the full version (www.rspb.org):

Five things to remember

- Avoid disturbing birds and their habitats – the birds' interests should always come first
- Be an ambassador for birdwatching
- Know the law and the rules for visiting the countryside, and follow them
- Send your sightings to the County Bird Recorder and the BirdTrack website (*a link is available on the RSPB website*)
- Think about the interests of wildlife and local people before passing on news of a rare bird, especially during the breeding season

The interests of birds come first

Birds respond to people in many ways, depending on the species, location and time of year.

Disturbance can keep birds from their nests, leaving chicks hungry or enabling predators to take eggs or young.

During cold weather or when migrants have just made a long flight, repeatedly flushing birds can mean they use up vital energy that they need for feeding. Intentional or reckless disturbance of some species at or near the nest is illegal in Britain.

Whether your particular interest is photography, ringing, sound-recording

DANCE OF THE DUNLINS

Another spectacle around the estuaries and coastline is an aerial dance sometimes performed by dunlins and knots, in which they twist and turn almost as one. This causes a flashing and strobing effect as the bold markings of the upper wings alternate with the paler undersides.

This is called a murmuration and typically occurs because the birds are trying to flee a predator or have been startled by the incoming tide. The best time to see this happen is as birds move toward the shore on the incoming tide, and although it may take many visits before success, it is well worth the effort. The name *Dance of the Dunlins* was coined by Doray Productions who produced a fabulous video of this behaviour that can be found online. Places where murmurations sometimes occur include near the RSPB's Campfield Marsh reserve on the Solway Firth, Cumbria Wildlife Trust's South Walney Nature Reserve, and the RSPB's Leighton Moss reserve on Morecambe Bay.

A better-known type of murmuration is that performed by starlings. These usually occur around dusk in late autumn and early winter. In Cumbria, sites where this behaviour has been seen in recent years include the countryside close to Gretna Green and at Southwaite Services on the M6 near Carlisle. The Leighton Moss reserve has spectacular displays in some years.

Dunlins on the Solway Firth showing their pale and dark plumage. The larger birds are lapwings and gulls ▼

WATCHING WATERBIRDS

With their bold markings and colours, wading birds and wildfowl are often photogenic subjects, especially when in large numbers, and the shoreline locations can make an interesting backdrop.

For larger birds, such as herons, geese or cormorants, a compact camera may suffice, but enthusiasts often use a camera with a zoom or prime lens. Ideally, if budgets allow, lenses would have a focal length of 400–500mm or more, but it is possible to get good results with less expensive equipment. Binoculars are a great help too when identifying birds. Most photographic shops can provide advice on the pros and cons of each approach.

Some of the best shots are obtained when there is a strong contrast between a bird's plumage and the background, such as black feathers against the sand, or a pale underbelly against the blue of the sea. Good lighting helps, ideally with the sun behind the photographer, and this may require an early start or an evening visit, depending on where a site is around the coast or estuary.

When watching birds, most are alert to movements on the horizon so it is best to remain at a distance, move slowly and try to keep out of sight. It is also important to avoid any type of disturbance that causes birds to take flight as it uses valuable energy, especially in winter, but also in the breeding season as it places eggs and chicks at risk from predators.

The Birdwatchers' Code gives useful advice to help avoid these kinds of problems. The Nature Photographers' Code of Practice from the Royal Photographic Society (www.rps.org) is another useful source of information.

Although it is rewarding to photograph the rarer species, it is worth being alert to other photographic opportunities. Even common species such as swans and gulls have their own beauty, particularly when in flight. The waterside locations mean that sunsets may be a bonus, together with the ever-changing appearance of the mudflats and sandbanks with the tides.

To learn more about birdwatching, it is worth joining a local group of the RSPB (www.rspb.org) or Cumbria Wildlife Trust (www.cumbriawildlifetrust.org.uk). Most arrange evening talks and weekend excursions, and some have access to areas open only to members.

Some nature reserves have visitor centres where staff and volunteers can give more information. Examples include the RSPB's Campfield Marsh reserve on the Solway Firth and the Cumbria Wildlife Trust's reserve at South Walney. Slightly further afield are the Wildfowl & Wetlands Trust reserve at Caerlaverock on the Solway Firth and the RSPB reserves at Mersehead on the Solway Firth and Leighton Moss on Morecambe Bay.

As with any activity near water, when watching waterbirds it is important to be aware of the risks from the tides and quicksand, and in particular never venture out onto saltmarshes, mudflats or sandbanks. The Introduction to this guide gives more tips on water safety.

This text is adapted from *The Mersey Estuary: A Travel Guide* by Kevin Sene

or birdwatching, remember that the interests of the bird must always come first.

Avoid going too close to birds or disturbing their habitats – if a bird flies away or makes repeated alarm calls, you're too close. And if it leaves, you won't get a good view.

Stay on roads and paths where they exist and avoid disturbing habitat used by birds.

Think about your fieldcraft. Disturbance is not just about going too close – a flock of wading birds on the foreshore can be disturbed from a mile away if you stand on the sea wall.

Repeatedly playing a recording of birdsong or calls to encourage a bird to respond can divert a territorial bird from other important duties, such as feeding its young. Never use playback to attract a species during its breeding season.

See the RSPB website for information on birds, habitats and the law in the UK.

Be an ambassador for birdwatching

Think about your fieldcraft and behaviour, not just so that you can enjoy your birdwatching, but so others can too.

Respond positively to questions from interested passers-by. They may not be birdwatchers yet, but a good view of a bird or a helpful answer may light a spark of interest. Your enthusiasm could start a lifetime's interest in birds and a greater appreciation of wildlife and its conservation.

Consider using local services, such as pubs, restaurants and petrol stations, and public transport. Raising awareness of the benefits to local communities of trade from visiting birdwatchers may, ultimately, help the birds themselves.

Respect for the countryside

Know the rules for visiting the countryside, and follow them.

Respect the wishes of local residents and landowners, and don't enter private land without permission unless it is open for public access on foot. Follow the codes on access and the countryside for the place you're walking in.

Irresponsible behaviour may cause a land manager to deny access to others (e.g. for necessary survey work). It may also disturb the bird or give birdwatching bad coverage in the media.

In England and Wales, access is to land mapped as mountain, moor, heath and down, and to registered common land. However, local restrictions may be in force, so follow the Countryside Code and plan your visit. In England, the Countryside Code and maps showing areas for public access are on the Government website (www.gov.uk).

Note: different regulations apply in Scotland, Wales and Northern Ireland.

▲ Grey heron (large): often seen waiting patiently at the shoreline to pounce on fish and easy to recognise in flight by its size, sharply curved neck and long trailing legs (Ravenglass Estuary)

Cormorant (large): near-black plumage and often seen standing at the water's edge – sometimes drying outstretched wings – or flying low above the surface singly or in small groups (Solway Firth) ▼

▲ Dunlin (small): grey-brown with a pale underbelly and black and white markings on the upper surface of the wings; famed for its spectacular murmurations (Solway Firth)

▲ Curlew (large): one of the largest wading birds with a grey-brown patterned body, downward curved bill and distinctive two-tone call that sounds a little like 'cur-lew'; increasingly endangered (Solway Firth)

Lapwing (large): black, dark-green and white plumage with a crest of feathers on the head; tend to fly in ragged circling formations and have stubbier wings than most wading birds; also known as the peewit after its distinctive breeding season call (near the Kent Estuary) ▼

▲ Barnacle goose (large): black neck and beak with mainly white face and belly. Patterned upper wings and black tail. Feeds in fields during the day and returns to the coast at dusk in large formations (Solway Firth)

TEN COMMON WATERBIRD SPECIES OF CUMBRIA AND THE LAKE DISTRICT

These are just a few examples of the most easily recognised types, and many other species are found around the shores of Cumbria.

The size entries indicate wingspans – Large >0.7m, Medium 0.4-0.7m, Small < 0.3m.

The descriptions indicate typical winter colours and can change significantly in the breeding season.

They also show where the photographs were taken. The Further Reading section suggests guides on bird identification and the RSPB website is another useful source of information.

▲ Redshank (medium): grey-brown mottled upper sides with pale undersides and bright orange-red legs that are its most distinctive feature when on the ground (Walney Island)

▲ Little egret (medium): small white heron with black legs and bill. Rarely seen in England before the 1990s, the species is now widespread (Leven Estuary)

Oystercatcher (large): bold black and white coloration, red-pink legs, a loud whistling/piping call and a distinctive orange-red beak often said to resemble a carrot (Ravenglass Estuary) ▼

Terns (medium): mainly white and grey with a black top to the head. Long slender wings and truly beautiful in flight. Little, common, sandwich and arctic terns are seen in Cumbria (Hodbarrow) ▼

Lake District fells viewed across Morecambe Bay

MORECAMBE BAY

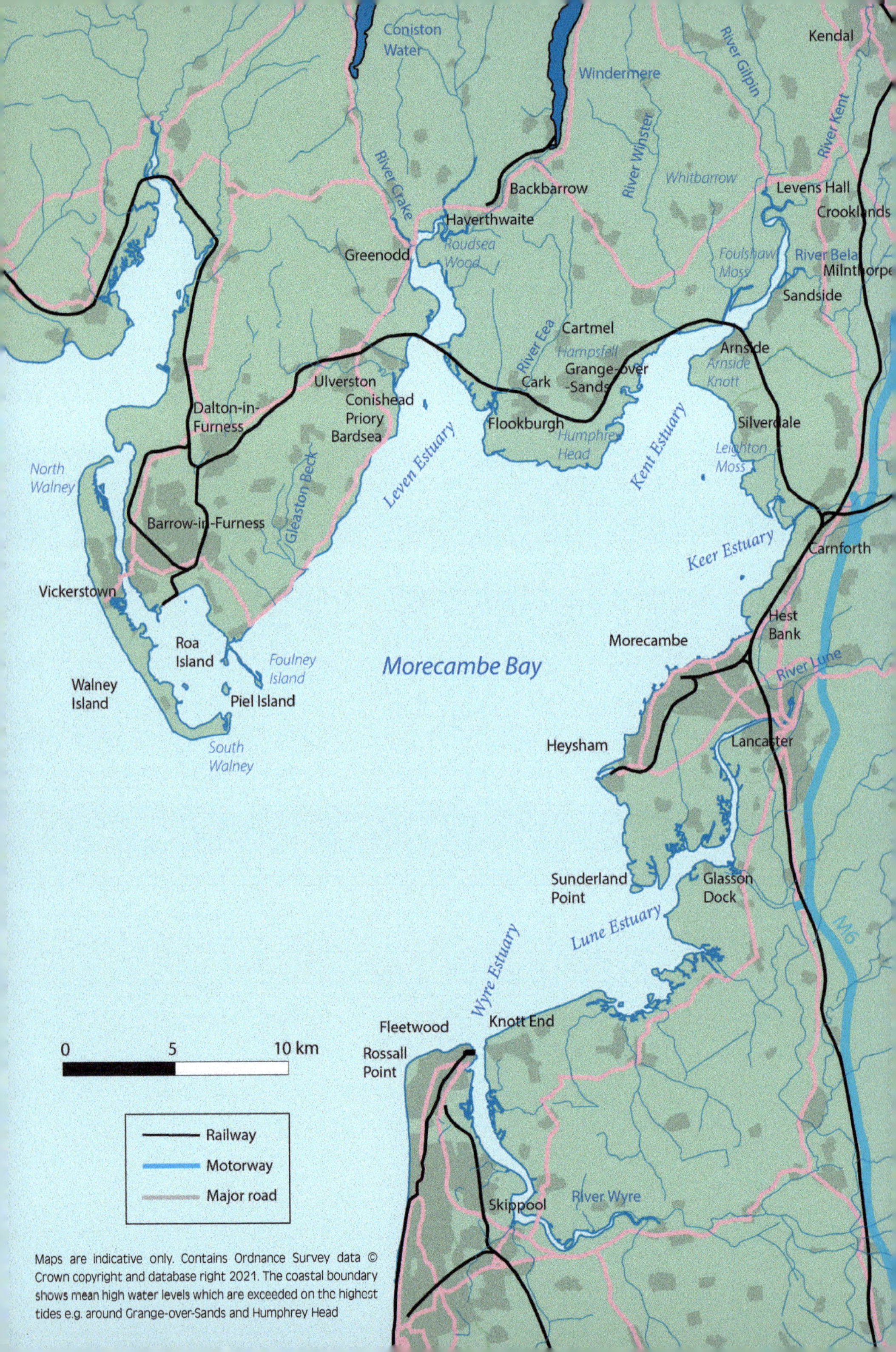

Maps are indicative only. Contains Ordnance Survey data © Crown copyright and database right 2021. The coastal boundary shows mean high water levels which are exceeded on the highest tides e.g. around Grange-over-Sands and Humphrey Head

▲ Morecambe Bay. In the foreground, Lancaster, Carnforth, Morecambe. On the other side of the estuary, Cartmel, Grange-over-Sands. At the entry to the bay, Milnthorpe. The far peninsula is Barrow-in-Furness (photo by Doc Searls).

Morecambe Bay extends from Fleetwood in the south to Walney Island in the north. It has the largest continuous intertidal area in the country, exposing up to 120 square miles of sandbanks and mudflats when the tide goes out.

It is a place of ever-changing scenery, on clear days with the bonus of a backdrop of distant Lake District fells. Around its shores are seaside resorts, stately homes and nature reserves, plus the city of Lancaster and the towns of Fleetwood, Morecambe, Ulverston and Barrow-in-Furness.

At low tide, the water's edge can reach several miles from the shore. Local fishermen travel far out into the bay, collecting the shrimps, cockles and mussels that thrive in its shallow waters. This is hazardous work as the tides rush in at several miles per hour and tidal bores form on the highest tides. Indeed, the tide is sometimes said to approach as fast as a galloping horse.

The bay has a rich maritime history and its estuaries were once major transport routes, bustling with sailing ships and steamships. During the industrial revolution the ports at Skippool, Lancaster, Milnthorpe and Greenodd were some of the busiest in the region. Many other wharves and piers dotted the shores of the bay.

Nowadays the main ports are in the deeper waters at Fleetwood, Heysham, Glasson Dock and Barrow-in-Furness. Shipping activity includes passenger ferries from Heysham, fishing boats from Fleetwood, naval shipbuilding at Barrow, and support vessels for the offshore windfarm and gas industries.

The bay is famed for its wildlife and in winter about a quarter of a million wading birds, ducks and geese congregate here. Species include oystercatchers, dunlins, curlews and redshanks. Other highlights include the ospreys that nest near the Kent Estuary and a seal colony at Walney Island.

Low limestone cliffs between Silverdale and the mouth of the Kent Estuary

LANCASHIRE SHORES

FEATURED LISTINGS

Bird's eye views	Williamson Park
Museums	Fleetwood
	Lancaster Maritime Museum
Maritime connections	Plover Scar Lighthouse
	St George's Quay
Wildlife	Leighton Moss
Ancient sites	St Patrick's Chapel
Seaside resorts	Fleetwood
	Morecambe
Tidal bore viewpoints	Skippool Creek
	Lancaster

THE CUMBRIA AND LAKE DISTRICT COAST

> **INTRODUCTION**
> The Lancashire shores of Morecambe Bay extend from Fleetwood to the Kent Estuary.
> Highlights include seaside resorts, coastal views, historic buildings and the city of Lancaster.
> The Port of Lancaster was once the busiest along its shores and ferries still depart from Heysham.
> Wildlife abounds including at the RSPB's flagship Leighton Moss reserve.

Places of interest

Fleetwood

The Lancashire shores of Morecambe Bay begin at Rossall Point at the western end of **Fleetwood**. This has long been an important navigational landmark and there was once a coastguard station here. This has now been replaced by the **Rossall Point** Observation Tower, a four-storey building that houses a volunteer coastal safety organisation. A viewing platform at the top is great for birdwatching and views across the bay; search for 'Rossall Point' at www.wyre.gov.uk for more information.

Fleetwood is a popular seaside resort and attractions along the sea front include a boating lake, a historic lighthouse and the Marine Hall Gardens (www.visitfleetwood.info). The town lies at the mouth of the River Wyre, which rises in the Forest of Bowland before flowing through Garstang and St Michael's on Wyre.

Commercial shipping in the Wyre Estuary began further upstream at Skippool Creek near Poulton-le-Fylde and at Wardleys Creek on the opposite shores. In the 18th century the port here was one of the busiest in northwest England with vessels departing for destinations all over the world.

As ship sizes increased, the winding channel of the Wyre became a barrier to expansion, so in the 19th century

Sunset over Morecambe Bay ▼

Fleetwood was chosen as a replacement. The gridded streets are the hallmark of a planned town and facilities included warehouses and a custom house. Trade was brisk and until World War I included scheduled services across the Irish Sea and pleasure steamers to Barrow to connect with trains to the Lake District. A deep-sea fishing industry continued until the 1970s.

Nowadays, the port has a busy marina and an inshore fishing fleet, although passenger services have ceased. To learn more about its history, **Fleetwood Museum**, in the former custom house, is an excellent place to visit (www.fleetwoodmuseum.co.uk).

Skippool is now home to a yacht club and is a good place to see the Wyre Tidal Bore. This forms on the highest tides and online footage suggests that it starts near Hambleton and sometimes reaches Cartford Bridge upstream. Chapter 1, Coastal Themes, describes how and when tidal bores form.

Fleetwood to the Lune Estuary

Heading east from Fleetwood, Knott End lies on the opposite shores of the Wyre Estuary. A ferry makes the short trip across the mouth of the estuary.

The shores of the bay are then mainly rural. Approaching the Lune Estuary, the ruins of 12th century **Cockersand Abbey** are a prominent landmark. The River Lune rises in the Yorkshire Dales near Kirkby Stephen; towns in its catchment include Sedbergh and Kirkby Lonsdale. The river has a Cumbrian connection as some of its tributaries rise in the Lake District.

▲ Partly developed tidal bore passing a wooden pier near Skippool Creek

▲ Lapwing near the mouth of the Lune Estuary

The tidal influence on the Lune extends into the city of Lancaster, which was once the largest port around Morecambe Bay. However, from the 19th century operations were increasingly moved to a deeper water facility at **Glasson Dock**. The dock is just inside the mouth of the estuary and as well as its busy marina it still handles cargo vessels. The village here is popular for its cafés and waterside walks and the Lune Estuary Path provides a pleasant cycling route from Lancaster.

Just offshore, Plover Scar Lighthouse was built at a similar time to Glasson Dock. This is operated by the Lancaster Port Commission along with another at the southern tip of Walney Island. In the days before radio and satellite, ship navigators would line up the Plover Scar light with that of the now-demolished Cockersand Lighthouse alongside the abbey to find their way into port.

Just inland from Glasson Dock, the estuary widens into an area of saltmarsh where it is joined by the River Conder. This is a popular area for birdwatching. The estuary narrows again on the final approach to **Lancaster**. Here the waterside promenades are popular with walkers and cyclists and several interesting interpretation panels describe the maritime history and wildlife of the estuary.

During the 18th century, St George's Quay was the heart of the port. Many of the elegant Georgian dock buildings remain and some have been converted to flats and offices. The former Custom House is now home to **Lancaster Maritime Museum**, which is an excellent place to find out more about the history of the port. Set over three floors, highlights include models of ships that used the port and displays on the transatlantic slave trade, the Lancaster Canal and the fishing industry in Morecambe Bay (www.lancaster.gov.uk).

On the highest tides, water levels rise and fall several metres at the Quay and the Lune Tidal Bore sometimes appears. This begins near the mouth of the estuary but dissipates beyond Glasson Dock, and is then at its best after reforming in the long, engineered channel that leads toward the city.

Possible viewpoints include the Golden Ball Hotel at Snatchems near the start of the channel and the promenade

Plover Scar Lighthouse ▼

MORECAMBE BAY | 63

▲ A partly developed tidal bore passing St George's Quay in Lancaster. The building with colonnades is the former custom house now home to Lancaster Maritime Museum

Lancaster Castle ▲

The city of Lancaster

As a major regional centre, Lancaster has many attractions beyond the estuary. From St George's Quay, footpaths lead to the impressive 12th century **Lancaster Castle**, which overlooks the city and the coastal plain (www.lancastercastle.com). This lies on Castle Hill alongside Lancaster Priory, where there has been a church since Saxon times. A Roman fort once stood here.

The nearby **Cottage Museum** is in an 18th century cottage giving insights into life in early Victorian times. The

opposite the maritime museum. On the best days, it reaches the Lune Millennium Bridge, a futuristic-looking footbridge that crosses the estuary. Chapter 1, Coastal themes, gives more details on how and when tidal bores form.

St George's Quay and the Lune Millennium Bridge ▼

Judges' Lodgings Museum is another place to visit, with fine art, antique furniture and childhood games dating back to the 17th century. It is housed in the city's oldest remaining town house. The Lancaster City Council website gives more information on both these museums and **Lancaster City Museum** (www.lancaster.gov.uk).

Perhaps the best views across Lancaster are from the area around **Lancaster Cathedral** (www.lancastercathedral.org.uk) and **Williamson Park**. The park is crowned by the Ashton Memorial, an impressive domed building looking out across Morecambe Bay toward distant Lake District fells. The extensive grounds include a tropical butterfly house, mini zoo and an elegant pavilion café (www.lancaster.gov.uk).

View of the Lake District fells across Morecambe Bay and the Lune Estuary from Williamson Park in Lancaster ▼

▲ Ashton Memorial in Williamson Park in Lancaster

THE PORT OF LANCASTER

Lancaster has a long tradition as a port, with the first regular shipments probably arriving in Roman times to supply the fort at Castle Hill.

Initially, Sunderland Point at the mouth of the estuary was used as a port, but in the 1750s local merchants funded development of channel improvements to the city, along with quays, warehouses and a custom house. The port soon grew to become the largest around Morecambe Bay, with destinations including Europe, the Americas and the Baltic States.

From the 1780s, new facilities at Glasson Dock allowed larger vessels to unload cargo for onward transport by smaller craft. Imported goods included cotton, rum and sugar, although sadly some merchants were involved in the slave trade. In 1826, the opening of a canal link from Glasson Dock to the city allowed ships to bypass the shifting channels of the Lune Estuary altogether, with onward connections along the Lancaster Canal to Kendal and Preston.

At first the canal company thrived, transporting coal, slate and limestone and taking finished goods to market. Passengers could travel between Kendal and Preston by horse-drawn packet boats in a few hours, benefiting from heated cabins and a stewarded galley service. There is a full-size display of one of these boats at Lancaster Maritime Museum along with a wealth of information about the history of the port.

Competition from the railways then led to a decline and the last freight load was carried in 1947. In Kendal the last few miles of the canal are now built over and used as a cycleway and footpath.

The rest of the canal is popular for leisure boating. During the tourist season volunteers from the Lancaster Canal Trust run narrowboat trips in the northern reaches, starting from the village of Crooklands. When the boat is operating, an exhibition on the history of the canal is open to visitors. This is located in the old boat stables opposite the Crooklands Hotel and includes updates on progress with restoring the last remaining sections north to Kendal (www.lctrust.co.uk).

Among the many impressive structures along the canal, the Lune Aqueduct, which carries the canal across the River Lune near Lancaster, stands out as a remarkable engineering achievement. There are fine views of the Lune from the top (www.canalrivertrust.org.uk). The magnificent Stainton Aqueduct near Crooklands has also been restored following storm damage in 2015, with work in progress to open the canal north toward Hincaster Tunnel, about five miles from Kendal.

The Lune Aqueduct ▶

The Cumbria and Lake District Coast

The Lune Estuary to Morecambe

On the northern shores of the Lune Estuary, opposite Glasson Dock, a picturesque line of houses looks out toward fishing boats and leisure craft moored offshore. This is **Sunderland Point**, which is reached by a road across the saltmarsh that floods at high tide. Before visiting, it is therefore essential to check tide tables and heed the warning signs.

The much-visited Sambo's Grave, a memorial to a slave put ashore nearby, lies just beyond the mouth of the estuary. On the highest tides, in the distance the Lune Tidal Bore is sometimes visible as a low wave making its way inland.

From Sunderland Point, the coastline is again mainly rural to the next landmark, which is Heysham Port, alongside the Heysham nuclear power station. Services include passenger ferries to the Isle of Man and cargo ships to Ireland.

Heysham village is a short way inland with picturesque 17th century cottages along its winding streets. The **Heysham Heritage Centre** describes its history (www.heyshamheritage.org.uk). The low headland of Heysham Head is a great place for views of the bay and the ruins of **St Patrick's Chapel** near the top are thought to date from the 8th century (www.nationaltrust.org.uk).

The popular seaside resort of **Morecambe** lies just to the east, with a wide choice of shops, cafés and restaurants and a busy year-round programme of festivals and events (www.visitlancashire.com).

Perhaps its best-known sight is the fabulous 1930s art deco Midland Hotel

▲ (Top to Bottom) Sunderland Point looking inland along the Lune Estuary; The access road to Sunderland Point at high tide. The sign reads 'DANGER beware of fast tides, hidden channels and quicksands'; Looking inland along the Keer Estuary from the coast

▲ The Refreshment Room at Carnforth Station Heritage Centre

on the promenade. The last remnant of the old harbour, known as the Stone Jetty, extends out from the shore nearby, with great views back to the town and along the coast. In addition to a lifeboat, the RNLI station here operates a hovercraft for rescues from the sands and mudflats. Planning is underway for Eden Project North, which will be built at the sea front to celebrate the wildlife and environment of Morecambe Bay, and be a northern counterpart of the Eden Project in Cornwall (www.edenproject.com).

The jetty and promenade feature some imaginative outdoor art. This includes a bronze statue of the comedian Eric Morecambe, who was born in the town, and a plaque indicating the names of distant Lake District peaks. Along the jetty, a Time and Tide Bell chimes with the rise and fall of the tide and is part of a national network designed to draw public attention to the threat of climate change (www.timeandtidebell.org). There was once a second pier to the north, with a pavilion and ballroom, but this was demolished in the 1990s.

Today Morecambe is home to fishing and leisure craft, but during the late 19th century a cargo and passenger service

St Patrick's Chapel ruins at Heysham Head ▶

operated from the Stone Jetty. A railway line ran along the jetty providing train connections for steamships bound for the Isle of Man, Dublin, Londonderry and Belfast. A wooden jetty, now demolished, stood nearby. The passenger service was transferred to Heysham in 1904 to be replaced by a shipbreaker's yard which operated for about thirty years. Nowadays it seems remarkable that the breakers were allowed to operate in a seaside resort.

Morecambe to the Kent Estuary

Heading north from Morecambe, the village of **Hest Bank** lies a short way beyond. In the 19th century this was the starting point for a scheduled stagecoach service across the sands, which is described in the section on the Kent Estuary. Until the mid-19th century, ships used to unload goods at a jetty here to be transported the short distance overland by horse and cart to the Lancaster Canal. Nowadays this is a popular spot to admire the coastal views and a great place for watching wading birds in the winter.

The Keer Estuary to the north is the smallest estuary around Morecambe Bay, as the tidal influence only reaches a short way inland. Its channel snakes across the sands at low tide and on the northern shores a low hill is a relic of the area's iron smelting past, and one of several landscaped slag heaps around Morecambe Bay and the Duddon Estuary. Despite their uninspiring origins, these can make good viewpoints and some are now wildlife havens, such as near Ulverston and Askam-in-Furness.

The River Keer rises close to the town of Kirkby Lonsdale and the main tourist destination along its course is **Carnforth**. This is an attractive market town and the **Carnforth Station Heritage Centre**, on a platform at the station, is a great place to find out about local and railway history (www.carnforthstation.co.uk).

It also features a more surprising display on the life and works of the British film director David Lean. His most famous film was the 1945 classic *Brief Encounter* and several scenes were shot at the station. Vintage suitcases and posters add to the atmosphere and visitors can dine at the Refreshment Room, which is a replica of a studio set used in the film.

Further north the RSPB's **Leighton Moss Nature Reserve** is an area of reed beds, coastal lagoons, limestone grassland and woodland close to Morecambe Bay (www.rspb.org.uk). It has the best facilities of any RSPB reserve in the region. The main part is slightly inland, with a visitor centre, observation tower, enclosed bird hides, a shop and a café. Highlights include otters, red deer, avocets, marsh harriers and bitterns. Spectacular starling murmurations occur in some years. About two miles away, an area of mudflats, lagoons and marsh at the coast is a refuge for waterbirds including redshanks, lapwings and oystercatchers. Self-guided walks and wildlife events are held year-round.

The RSPB visitor centre is a short walk from the railway station in the attractive village of **Silverdale**. Limestone pavement and low cliffs are a feature of the coast nearby, including at the coastal site of Jack Scout, which is another great place for watching waterbirds, as is **Jenny Brown's Point** to the south,

MORECAMBE BAY | 69

where an unusual limestone brick tower was associated with a short-lived iron and copper smelting venture in the 18th century. The stately home of **Leighton Hall** is another nearby attraction (www.leightonhall.co.uk).

Heading north, the next major landmark is Arnside Knott, which lies in Cumbria. This marks the start of the Kent Estuary, which is described in the following section. There is also a description of sights within the Arnside and Silverdale AONB, which extends as far south as the Keer Estuary and includes several nature reserves in Lancashire.

▲ Yachts on Morecambe Bay

▼ Coastal views near Jenny Brown's Point

The Kent Estuary viewed from Arnside

KENT ESTUARY

FEATURED LISTINGS

Bird's eye views	Hampsfell
	Arnside Knott
	Humphrey Head
Maritime connections	Arnside Pier
Wildlife	Arnside Knott
	Foulshaw Moss
Historic buildings	Levens Hall
	Cartmel Priory
Waterside walks & seaside resorts	Arnside
	Grange-over-Sands
Tidal bore viewpoints	Arnside

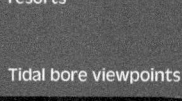

THE CUMBRIA AND LAKE DISTRICT COAST

> **INTRODUCTION**
> The Kent Estuary is the second largest around Morecambe Bay and one of its most scenic.
> On its southeastern shores the village of Arnside is a pleasant place to wander. Over the water Grange-over-Sands has been a holiday resort since Victorian times and historic Cartmel and its 12th century priory is nearby.
> Viewpoints for the estuary include Arnside Knott, Hampsfell and spectacular Humphrey Head, a limestone promontory jutting out from the shoreline.
> Other highlights include the stately home of Levens Hall and the ospreys of Foulshaw Moss Nature Reserve. On the highest tides, Arnside's tidal bore attracts many visitors.

Places of interest

Southeast shores

The Kent Estuary is one of the largest and most picturesque around Morecambe Bay. Heading north from Silverdale, it begins in the general area of Blackstone Point near Arnside and extends to Humphrey Head on the opposite shore. The low tide channel of the River Kent flows far out into Morecambe Bay.

Blackstone Point is an area of low limestone cliffs and shingle beach. A short way inland is a holiday park, from where a minor road leads to Arnside.

The Promenade in **Arnside** is a pleasant place to wander with scenic

(Top to Bottom) Arnside waterfront; Deer at the grounds of Dallam Tower alongside the River Bela; The Arnside Bore ▶

Limestone cliffs at Whitbarrow, near the top of the Kent Estuary ▶

views across the estuary, including of the viaduct that carries the coastal railway to Grange-over-Sands. There is a good choice of shops, pubs and cafés.

Arnside was once a port and the pier still remains. It is a popular viewpoint for one of the town's more unusual attractions, the Arnside Bore, a spectacular wave that travels inland on the highest tides. There are also great views of the estuary from the nearby hill of **Arnside Knott** (159m).

Heading upstream, the coastal road briefly leaves the estuary shore, rejoining it after passing the residential area of Storth. Sailing ships once berthed at the small settlement of Sandside and the Ship Inn pub is a reminder of those times. The road occasionally floods in this area on the highest tides.

The grounds of **Dallam Tower** are alongside the River Bela, which is a tributary of the Kent Estuary. The stately home here is private but there is a footpath

Saltmarsh viewed at low tide from the promenade at Grange-over-Sands. Holme Island in the distance is privately owned and reached via a causeway ▼

through the surrounding parkland, with its resident deer population. In the 18th century, the river was the centre of activity for the port of Milnthorpe, once one of the busiest ports around Morecambe Bay.

From Dallam Tower it is just a short way to **Milnthorpe**, an attractive market town with a traditional market square. The top of the Kent Estuary lies upstream of its meeting point with the River Bela, close to the stately home of **Levens Hall**. Built in Elizabethan times, the drawing room, grand hall and dining hall are open to the public.

The formal gardens were established in the 17th century and include many examples of topiary, with yew and box trees cut into elaborate abstract and geometrical shapes. Other highlights include a gift shop and a popular kitchen café (www.levenshall.co.uk).

The hall lies close to the banks of the Kent and, on the highest tides, the tidal influence in the river sometimes extends upstream. **Sizergh Castle** is nearby, another stately home with beautiful

Cartmel Priory ▲
An unusual view of Humphrey Head from minor roads near Allithwaite ▼

gardens and parkland. Facilities include a shop and café (www.nationaltrust.org.uk).

Northwest shores

The opposite shores of the Kent Estuary lie on the Cartmel Peninsula. Some road signs refer to this as one of the Lake District Peninsulas, the other being the Furness Peninsula to the west.

Heading toward the coast, much of the shoreline is fringed by saltmarsh. The low cliffs of **Whitbarrow** (215m) are nearby and their weathered limestone sometimes takes on a spectacular glow in the sunshine. The limestone pavement and soils at the summit support a wide range of rare plant and insect species, and lie within the Whitbarrow Hervey Memorial Reserve (www.cumbriawildlifetrust.org.uk).

Two tributaries join the Kent Estuary in this area, the River Gilpin and the River Winster. However, the shoreline is largely inaccessible and minor roads lead to farmhouses and the small village of Meathop, rather than to the waterside. **Foulshaw Moss** and **Meathop Moss** nature reserves lie on the remnants of the lowland peat bog that once fringed these shores, and ospreys have successfully raised chicks at Foulshaw Moss in recent years.

The next place with easy access to the shoreline is **Grange-over-Sands**. This is the largest town around the estuary. Originally a small fishing village, it became a popular coastal resort in the mid-19th century when the new railway from Lancaster to Barrow-in-Furness brought in wealthy tourists to enjoy the sea air.

The wide promenade is still a great place for views of the estuary although is

Cartmel Priory Gatehouse ▲

now fringed by saltmarsh rather than a beach due to changes in the path of the river channel. There are plans to restore the art deco Grange Lido to its former glory.

The Ornamental Gardens near the station include a lake with a resident population of native, migratory and ornamental ducks and geese, while an elegant arcade nearby includes tea rooms and speciality shops.

From Grange, the promenade and minor roads lead to the village of Kents Bank, further toward the coast. This is close to the impressive limestone promontory of **Humphrey Head**, which is another great viewpoint for the area and marks the end of this side of the estuary.

The historic town of **Cartmel** lies about two miles inland on the banks of

COASTAL VIEWPOINTS

Three hills around the Kent Estuary provide some of the finest coastal views in Cumbria.

On the southern shores, Arnside Knott (159m) lies close to Arnside and road signs indicate the way. From the National Trust car park a climb through woods and grassland leads to the top. A plaque near the parking area shows the directions to distant Lake District fells and other landmarks including the railway viaduct across the estuary and the Howgills in the Yorkshire Dales (www.nationaltrust.org.uk).

From the top it is possible to continue to Far Arnside and return to Arnside along coastal paths, taking extra care along clifftop sections. However, the sands and mudflats are best avoided due to the risks of quicksand and because they become rapidly submerged as the tide comes in. Check tide times first before setting off.

Hampsfell (222m) lies near Grange-over-Sands on the opposite shores. This is another low-lying fell with superb views of the estuary and the Lake District. Due to grazing, its slopes are more open than on Arnside Knott, with just the occasional patch of trees and scrub. Footpaths lead from Grange-over-Sands or from minor roads nearby, if you can find a suitable parking spot.

At the top, an unusual sight is a square stone building with a viewing platform on the roof. This was built as a shelter for travellers and is known as The Hospice. The views from here take in Arnside Knott and the coast toward Morecambe, parts of the Leven Estuary and peaks in the Lake District too. A circular viewfinder shows the direction to local landmarks and distant fells.

Close to the mouth of the estuary, Humphrey Head (53m) is another great viewpoint. This unusual limestone promontory juts out into Morecambe Bay with impressive cliffs on its western side.

The grass-covered slopes along the crest include some much-photographed hawthorn trees, their branches outstretched in the direction of the prevailing wind. There are fine views across the Kent Estuary and Morecambe Bay, and toward the mouth of the Leven Estuary.

The main car parking area is at the end of the access road beneath the cliffs: be sure to park above high tide level. The usual route to the top begins before that, with an information board showing the way. The path beyond the parking area beneath the cliffs should not be taken due to the risks from quicksand and the tide, which comes in surprisingly fast here.

The types of wildlife seen at Humphrey Head and Arnside Knott are described later in this section.

Arnside viewed from Hampsfell ▼

▲ Railway viaduct over the Kent Estuary viewed from Arnside Knott, with Whitbarrow in the distance

Morecambe Bay viewed from Hampsfell, from near Blackstone Point to Jenny Brown's Point ▼

SOURCE TO SEA: RIVER KENT

The River Kent rises in an impressive valley above the small village of Kentmere surrounded by high mountain peaks. The route around the top is one of the finest horseshoe walks in the Lake District, with one of its high points the unusually named Ill Bell (757m). Slate was once quarried in the valley and Kentmere Reservoir was constructed to supply the many watermills further downstream.

The first major settlement is Staveley where the Kent is joined by the River Gowan. Staveley Mill Yard, site of a former mill, is now a major tourist attraction with shops, including a bike store, offices, a brewery and a café popular with hillwalkers (www.staveleymillyard.com). About three miles downstream, the River Sprint joins the Kent to be followed by the River Mint in Kendal. It is perhaps just a coincidence that the town's most famous export, Kendal Mint Cake, is made in a factory nearby.

Kendal is the largest town in the catchment and visitor attractions include the Brewery Arts Centre, the Quaker Tapestry Museum, and the ruins of Kendal Castle on a hill overlooking the town. Abbott Hall on the banks of the Kent dates from the 18th century and now houses an art gallery and the Museum of Lakeland Life & Industry is nearby (www.visit-kendal.co.uk). The town has a wide choice of cafés, restaurants and shops and an active programme of events, including the Kendal Mountain Festival, which draws adventurers from around the world (www.kendalmountainfestival.com).

Leaving Kendal, the Kent flows past farmland before passing through a series of rapids in a narrow gorge and then over Force Falls, close to Sedgwick. The Kent Estuary begins just past Levens Hall, although on the highest tides the tidal influence extends upstream of the A6 road bridge over the river.

The River Bela (pronounced 'Bee-lah') joins downstream on the southeastern shores. Its high point is on Lambrigg Fell (339m) to the east of Kendal. A restored corn mill at Beetham (www.heronmill.org) is a reminder of the many watermills once found along the river. A recent hydropower installation that powers the site provides an interesting contrast with the restored 18th century waterwheel and machinery.

The largest town along the Bela is Milnthorpe. About a mile beyond, the river passes over a weir to join the estuary. This weir is occasionally overtopped on the highest tides, which can lead to tidal flooding of the main road alongside Dallam Tower Park.

Two other rivers join the estuary on its opposite shores upstream from Grange-over-Sands. These are the Gilpin and the Winster and both rise to the east of Windermere, where the highest point is about 250m above sea level. They then flow either side of the long limestone ridge of Whitbarrow. The Gilpin passes through the Lyth Valley and, unusually for Cumbria, this has artificially drained areas for irrigation. Peat was once extracted here and damson orchards are widespread, with an annual Damson Day in April.

In its lowermost reaches the Gilpin passes through tide gates installed to reduce the risk from tidal flooding and then crosses saltmarsh to reach the estuary shores. The Winster once had a wide shallow tidal inlet that extended inland toward Lindale, with Holme Island at its mouth. The inlet was cut off with the construction of the coastal railway and the Winster now flows into the Kent Estuary along a narrow channel that passes beneath the railway.

Kendal Castle ▶

Kentmere Reservoir viewed from the Kentmere Horseshoe (Inset) The River Bela as it approaches the Kent Estuary

the River Eea. The skyline is dominated by 12th century **Cartmel Priory**, which along with its fortified gatehouse was saved from destruction following the dissolution of the monasteries (www.cartmelpriory.org.uk). The remains of the priory have served as the parish church ever since. The Cistercian Way long-distance footpath connects the priory with Furness Abbey near Barrow-in-Furness, which also dates from medieval times.

The gatehouse leads to the market square and other attractions in the town include its winding cobbled streets and the many cafés, pubs and restaurants. These include the Cartmel Village Shop where the famous Cartmel Sticky Toffee Pudding was first made and is still sold. Cartmel Racecourse is popular with racegoers and occasionally hosts open-air concerts.

Maritime history

The Kent Estuary has long been used to transport goods and people, with evidence of Viking settlement.

During the late 16th century, Milnthorpe became established as one of the largest ports around Morecambe Bay. Ships would be beached on mudflats in the tidal reaches of the River Bela for goods to be unloaded onto horse-drawn carts.

The port served the needs of Kendal and the surrounding area. A lively trade developed in locally produced gunpowder, textiles and grain, along with raw materials such as coal, salt, timber and pig iron, which could be melted down into iron products. Guano, derived from the droppings of sea birds and bats, was imported for use as a fertiliser and in making gunpowder.

At its peak, trade extended as far as Liverpool, Scotland, Ireland and the Baltic States. The port's decline began in the early 1800s when the Lancaster Canal was extended to Kendal, providing an alternative route to the town.

The increasing demand for deeper water facilities also led to a shift in activity down the estuary to Sandside. A popular pub, the Ship Inn, is a reminder of that time.

When the railway viaduct was built in the mid-19th century, it restricted ship access upstream, so Arnside became the main port, having previously been mainly a fishing village. However, trade had already much reduced by then, although some continued into the late 19th century, including from a quay at Blackstone Point near the mouth of the estuary. The pier in Arnside dates from this period, and pleasure steamers would occasionally stop there en route to other ports around Morecambe Bay. Traditional Morecambe Bay prawn fishing boats

Arnside Pier ▼

MORECAMBE BAY | 81

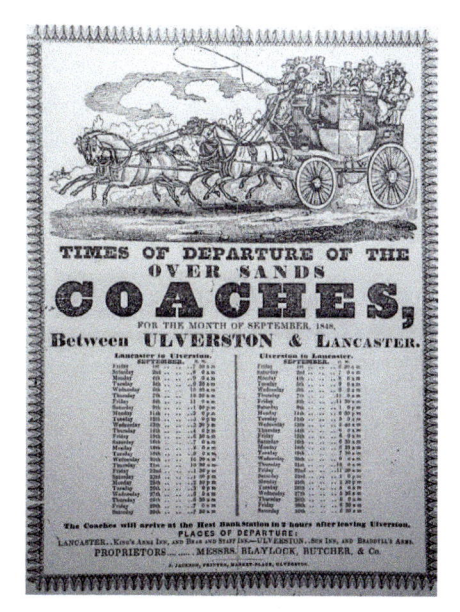

▲ A poster advertising stagecoach crossings of Morecambe Bay in the 19th century (© Lancaster Museums)

– Lancashire Nobbies – were built in Arnside until the 1950s.

On the opposite shores, Grange-over-Sands also began as a fishing village, although Cartmel Priory traded grain by sea from there until the dissolution of the monasteries in the 16th century. Then, as the industrial revolution gained pace, ships were built locally on the tidal inlet of the River Winster, including a model to test the design for one of the world's first iron boats.

By the late 19th century, coastal steamers brought visitors to Grange from Morecambe and Fleetwood, berthing at one of two wooden piers. The piers are now long gone and in recent decades the course of the estuary channels has changed, so the promenade is now largely inaccessible to ships and boats.

Crossing the sands

Before the advent of the railways, Morecambe Bay was an obvious shortcut for merchants and travellers, rather than using the rough tracks around its shores. The lowland peat bogs that once fringed the northern shores added to the difficulties. However, rowing boats and

Walkers crossing the sands on an organised charity walk across the Kent Estuary ▼

sailing ships were subject to the vagaries of the winds and the tides, making a reliable service impractical.

Instead, the usual approach was to travel directly over the sands and the main route was across the mouth of the Kent Estuary. Some travellers would then continue across the Cartmel Peninsula and over the sands of the Leven Estuary to Ulverston.

This was a risky undertaking requiring expert guides who were provided by the priories at Furness, Cartmel and Conishead. Following the dissolution of the monasteries, guides were then appointed by the Duchy of Lancaster. Traders would typically use packhorses or horse-drawn wagons with wealthier travellers riding horses or using lightweight carriages such as gigs. Many others travelled on foot, particularly on the shorter crossing of the Leven Estuary.

From the 1780s to the 1850s there was a scheduled passenger service between Lancaster and Ulverston. This began with lightweight carriages, but stagecoaches drawn by four horses were used in later years.

The usual route was to depart overland from Lancaster for Hest Bank to the north, and then to make the journey of several miles across the Keer and Kent estuaries to Kents Bank. From there, the route crossed the Cartmel Peninsula to Sand Gate near Flookburgh before taking to the sands again in the Leven Estuary. The route here passed Chapel Island, which could be used as a place of refuge if the tides were approaching, before reaching the shore again near Ulverston.

▲ Traditional laurel branch route marker on a Cross Bay Walk

The journey between Ulverston and Hest Bank took two hours and departure times were varied to fit in with the tides. The website of the Hest Bank inn, now a popular pub, and once known as the Sands Inn (www.hestbankinn.co.uk), notes that:

By 1812, at the height of the coaching trade, a lantern room had been constructed to guide travellers over the sands to the inn, and the stables were extended; they could now hold 16 horses and four drivers, as well as a rescue team for the treacherous Morecambe Crossing.

One of the main duties of guides was to mark out the route with branches of laurel, which due to the shifting sands needed to be done every day. This is a tradition that continues on the charitable Cross Bay Walks across the Kent Estuary. These are organised walks accompanied by an expert guide and millions of pounds have been raised this way. Due to the stunning views

THE ARNSIDE BORE

Several of the estuaries around Cumbria have tidal bores and the Arnside Bore is perhaps the best known, becoming a local tourist attraction.

The most popular viewpoint is from the pier alongside the main promenade in Arnside. A coin-operated telescope allows a closer view. Often the first sign of the bore's approach is a white line of surf in the distance and the speed and power of its approach is most impressive to see.

The tidal bore forms in the general area of Blackstone Point. After passing the pier it tends to dissipate on passing the bridge piers but on the highest tides it can reach Sandside, further upstream, and sometimes even the mouth of the River Bela.

At Arnside water levels typically rise several metres in the hour or so after the tidal bore passes. Many people have been caught out by the tides, and the coastguard station at Arnside has a rescue boat available. During the main tourist season the council sounds a warning siren twice as the tide advances, with the first blast about 15 to 20 minutes before it arrives in Arnside and the second shortly after it passes Blackstone Point. If conditions are right, the tidal bore appears within minutes of the second blast. As with any natural phenomenon, sightings are not guaranteed but the nearby cafés, pubs and waterside walks are a great compensation.

Warning sign at Arnside ▲

If travelling by car, be aware that the waterside car park can flood in extreme tides, so take care if lingering after the bore has passed. It is also important to choose a safe viewing location above the high water level, such as the pier, and never venture out onto the sands and mudflats. Chapter 1, Coastal themes, has more information on water safety and finding out tide and tidal bore timings.

▼ The Arnside Tidal Bore viewed from Arnside (left) and Sandside (right)

and challenging terrain, even seasoned hill walkers sometimes describe these trips as one of the most remarkable days out they have had in Cumbria.

The normal route is from Arnside to Kents Bank and walks typically take several hours, going a surprisingly long way out into Morecambe Bay to find a safe place to wade across the channel of the Kent. For safety, a tractor trailer is on hand to carry any participants who require help.

Guides have the title of Queen's Guide to the Sands and since 1877 have been appointed by the Guide over Sands Trust, which was set up as a charity by the Duchy of Lancaster (www.guideoversands.co.uk). The current guide of the Leven sands is Raymond Porter.

For the Kent sands, Michael Wilson is the 26th to have this honour. Perhaps the most famous is his immediate predecessor, Cedric Robinson MBE, who held the role for more than fifty years before retiring in 2019. Like most previous guides, both gained their intimate working knowledge of the bay as fishermen, setting nets out for shrimps, whitebait, cockles and flat-fish.

Cedric has published several books on his experiences, which included guiding celebrities and VIPs across the sands, one of whom was Prince Philip, the Duke of Edinburgh.

Wildlife

Morecambe Bay is famed for its birdwatching opportunities and the Kent Estuary is no exception. Saltmarsh extends along much of the shoreline, and the mudflats provide rich feeding for migratory waterbirds, such as oystercatchers, dunlins and redshanks. The best viewpoints are toward the mouth of the estuary. As always, viewing should be from a safe location, away from the risks of quicksand and the tides.

The River Kent is renowned for salmon and sea trout, which pass through the estuary on their way upstream. Spotting salmon is a challenge but there are some great photographs online of

Canada geese where the River Bela meets the Kent Estuary ▼

fish leaping Force Falls. An information board at Stramongate Weir in Kendal suggests that salmon are sometimes seen there. Fish passes further upstream help fish to reach spawning grounds higher in the catchment.

There are several nature reserves and conservation areas around the estuary, including the Arnside and Silverdale Area of Outstanding Natural Beauty (AONB) on its southeastern shores. This is described below along with the two largest reserves around the estuary: Foulshaw Moss and Humphrey Head.

Other reserves include Brown Robin and Meathop Moss. **Brown Robin** lies on limestone slopes above Grange-over-Sands and is known for woodland walks and spring displays of wildflowers. In contrast, **Meathop Moss** has some of the best-preserved lowland raised mires in Cumbria, as does nearby Foulshaw Moss.

Arnside and Silverdale AONB

An AONB is an area which has been designated for conservation due to its impressive wildlife and landscape. The area south of the Kent Estuary is one such place and the Arnside and Silverdale AONB was established in 1972 and extends south into Lancashire as far as the Keer Estuary (www.arnsidesilverdaleaonb.org.uk).

It is managed from an office in Arnside at the old station building alongside the railway station, and an information centre gives background on the history and wildlife of the area. Highlights include the historic villages of Beetham, Silverdale and Warton and the many walks through ancient

▲ Oystercatchers seen from Arnside with the cliffs of Whitbarrow in the distance

woods and over limestone hills, some with great views of Morecambe Bay. Nature reserves inland include those at Trowbarrow, Warton Crag and Gait Barrows, while coastal sights include the RSPB's flagship reserve at Leighton Moss. This is described in the section on Morecambe Bay along with two other great birdwatching sites, Jack Scout and Jenny Brown's Point. Ospreys from the Foulshaw Moss Nature Reserve are often seen at Leighton Moss and in the Kent Estuary.

Perhaps the best-known feature is Arnside Knott, whose main walks are described earlier in this chapter. This is a Site of Special Scientific Interest (SSSI) known for its wildflowers in the spring and abundant insect and birdlife, including buzzards which are often seen overhead. Many unusual plant species thrive in its limestone soils, including wild orchids, and the mix of plants is conducive to butterflies, which breed in large numbers in the summer. These include the Scotch Argus and the rare high brown fritillary, although both are in decline.

The area is managed for conservation by the National Trust, creating a patchwork of habitat which contributes to the extraordinarily varied mix of species found here. This work includes protecting the remaining areas of ancient woodland.

The objectives of the AONB are supported by the Landscape Trust, a charitable organisation which owns and maintains some reserves and organises walks, lectures, exhibitions and practical conservation tasks (www.landscapetrust.org.uk). The Trust also publishes the *Keer to Kent* journal three times a year, which is a great source of information on the wildlife and habitat of the area.

Foulshaw Moss

The coastal plain of south Cumbria was once fringed with areas of peat bog known as lowland raised mires. These were formed over thousands of years as sphagnum mosses collected in hollows and their remains were compacted by the weight of layers above.

Wading birds at sunset near Sandside ▼

The Foulshaw Moss Nature Reserve includes some of the last remaining mosses in this area. Although damaged by drainage and conifer planting in the 1950s and 1960s, the mosses are now being restored by Cumbria Wildlife Trust, who manage the reserve (www.cumbriawildlifetrust.org.uk).

From a display area at the entrance, raised boardwalks lead across the restored areas, passing ponds and an area of wet woodland. These are a haven for dragonflies and other insects, with a viewing platform alongside one of the largest ponds looking out across the reserve.

Many rare species of plant grow on the mosses, including the insect-eating sundew. These plants provide shelter and food for nesting birds, which in turn attract birds of prey. For example, buzzards, red kites and marsh harriers are often seen around the reserve. There is a resident herd of red deer.

In recent years the reserve has become famed for a pair of ospreys that breed there. These were enticed to nest by building a wooden nesting platform and have successfully raised several chicks. The nest, which lies in a row of Scots pines, is just visible with binoculars from the viewing platform. Webcam images streamed to the Trust's website provide close-up views during the breeding season, which lasts through

(Top to bottom) A pair of osprey chicks on the nest at Foulshaw Moss (© Cumbria Wildlife Trust); General view of Foulshaw Moss Nature Reserve with Whitbarrow in the distance; Dragonfly at a pond at Foulshaw Moss Nature Reserve ▶

spring and summer. The adult ospreys can sometimes be seen fishing in the Kent Estuary or at the RSPB's Leighton Moss reserve.

Chapter 1, Coastal themes, gives more background both on how peat bogs form and the remarkable life cycle of the osprey.

Humphrey Head

Like Arnside Knott, as well as being a fine viewpoint, Humphrey Head is a SSSI. It is managed by Cumbria Wildlife Trust. Habitat includes grassland and the cliffs to the west and nearby Humphrey Head Wood, which is just outside the reserve.

In winter it can be a good spot to watch wading birds such as curlews, oystercatchers and redshanks as they move ahead of the advancing tide. The cliffs are a nesting site for peregrine falcons which are occasionally seen wheeling high above. The grassland at the top is grazed but kept fertiliser free, which helps to improve the range of plant species found, which include wildflowers in the spring.

The walk to the top provides fine views of Morecambe Bay and surrounding hills, but as noted earlier, the surrounding sands and mudflats are potentially dangerous due to the tides and quicksand.

Hawthorn tree at Humphrey Head ▼

Morecambe Bay at low tide from Humphrey Head ▶

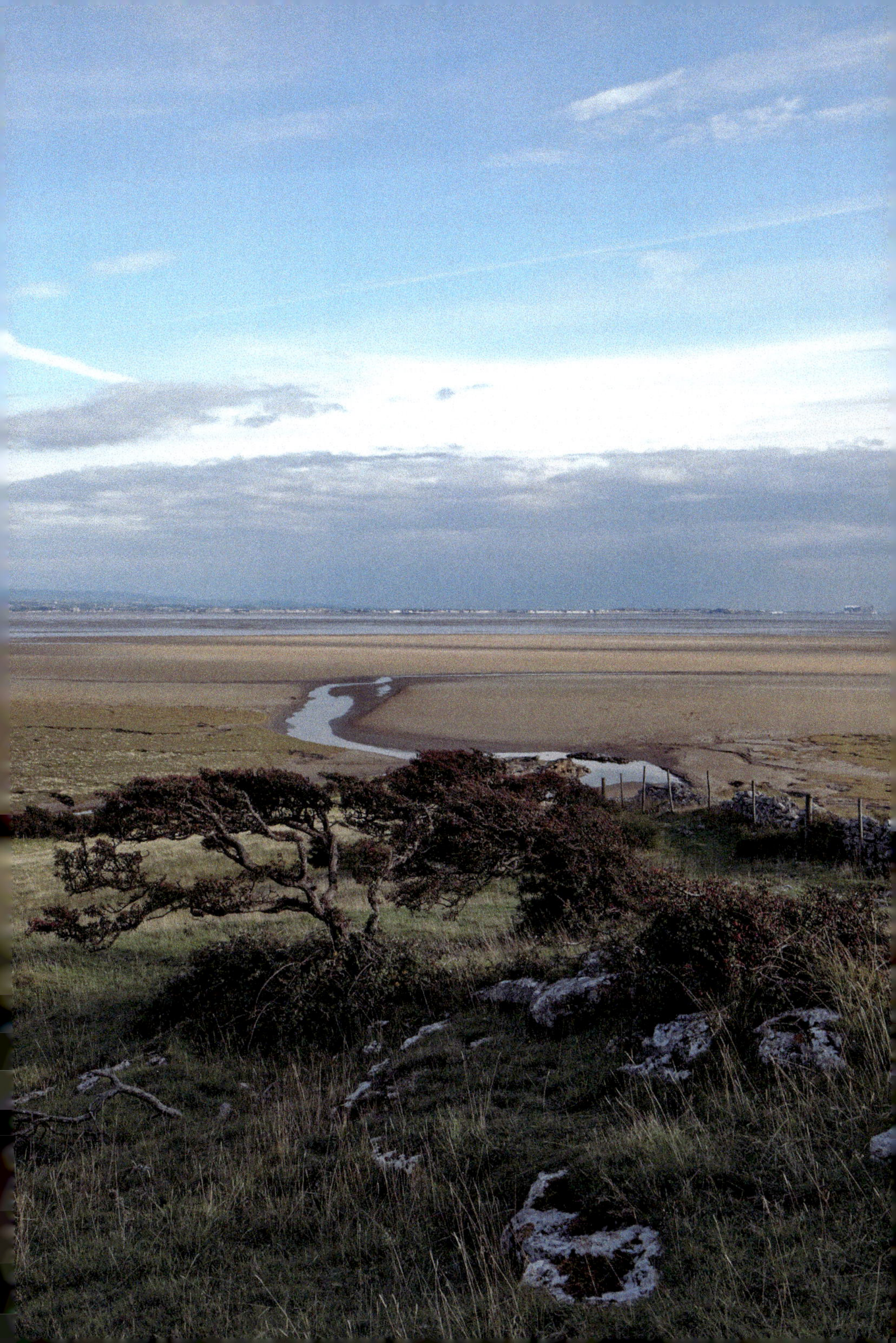

Leven Estuary from Hoad Hill in Ulverston

LEVEN ESTUARY
and Furness Peninsula

FEATURED LISTINGS

Bird's eye views	Sir John Barrow Monument
Museums	The Dock Museum
Maritime connections	Canal Foot, Ulverston
	Piel Castle
	Walney Lighthouse
Wildlife	Foulney Island
	South Walney Island
Historic buildings	Holker Hall
	Conishead Priory
Ancient sites	Birkrigg Stone Circle
	Furness Abbey
	Piel Castle
Waterside walks	Canal Foot, Ulverston
	Roa Island
	South Walney Island
Tidal bore viewpoints	Canal Foot, Ulverston

THE CUMBRIA AND LAKE DISTRICT COAST

INTRODUCTION
The Leven Estuary is the largest in south Cumbria and lies between the Cartmel and Furness peninsulas. Further south, the Furness Peninsula ends near Roa Island, on the shores of Morecambe Bay.

Sights around the estuary and bay include historic towns, museums, nature reserves and a Buddhist monastery

Shipbuilding still thrives at Barrow-in-Furness and there are many reminders of the area's maritime past, including the Ulverston Canal and Piel Castle.

The islands near Barrow are a haven for wildlife, including a seal population, as are the extensive areas of woodland and saltmarsh further upstream.

Places of interest

Humphrey Head to Haverthwaite

The Leven Estuary is the largest around Morecambe Bay and is flanked by the Cartmel Peninsula to the east and the Furness Peninsula to the west. It meets the Kent Estuary around Humphrey Head.

The attractive village of **Flookburgh** is close to Humphrey Head, with traditional whitewashed cottages and a market square. Fishing remains an important activity on Morecambe Bay, using tractors to set nets for delicacies such as cockles, mussels and prawns. Cartmel Sticky Toffee Pudding is made here, which is sold to stores and supermarkets worldwide.

(Top to Bottom) The River Eea at Cark-in-Cartmel; A Skydive Northwest aircraft taking off from Cark Airfield with the cliffs of Humphrey Head in the background; View from Sand Gate across the Leven Estuary with Ulverston in the distance ▶

MORECAMBE BAY | 93

A Lakeside and Haverthwaite Railway train passes alongside the River Leven (© Lakeside and Haverthwaite Railway)

The River Leven at the Grade II listed Backbarrow Bridge

Cark Airfield is close by and is home to a busy parachute club. Beginners can make tandem jumps with an experienced instructor from high above Morecambe Bay (www.skydivenorthwest.co.uk).

Heading up the estuary, it is joined by the unusually named River Eea at Sand Gate, where there is a scattering of farm buildings. The picturesque village of **Cark-in-Cartmel** is a short way upstream with traditional pubs and a former watermill, which is now a private residence.

Holker Hall lies just outside Cark. Built in the 16th century, the house is open to the public along with its award-winning gardens. Deer graze in the surrounding parkland. The busy schedule of events runs year-round and there is a gift shop, courtyard café and restaurant (www.holker.co.uk).

Beyond Sand Gate, access to the shoreline is more limited, with farms, conifer plantations and a private holiday park. Perhaps the best way to see this area is from the coastal railway, with particularly fine views from the viaduct across the estuary. Long-distance coastal walkers typically head inland here, following the low line of hills along the west of the Cartmel Peninsula.

The first road bridge across the estuary is near the village of Haverthwaite and the tidal influence normally begins just downstream from this crossing. From the bridge, a minor road follows the shores of the Leven to **Roudsea Wood and Mosses** National Nature Reserve, which is described later.

▲ The waterside café of the Lakeland Motor Museum viewed across the River Leven (© Lakeland Motor Museum)

Haverthwaite area

The village of **Haverthwaite** lies near the start of the Leven Estuary and is close to two of the most popular tourist attractions in the Lake District. These are the **Lakeside & Haverthwaite Railway** and the Lakeland Motor Museum.

The railway terminus is next to the A590 coastal road and steam trains leave from here for Lakeside at the southern end of Windemere, the largest lake in the Lake District (www.lakesiderailway.co.uk). Attractions at Lakeside include cafés, restaurants and the Lakes Aquarium. It is a boarding point for ferry trips around the lake.

The railway was once a branch line of the coastal railway and continued as far as Ulverston. It was taken into private ownership in the 1970s. There is a café and gift shop at the station and the main engine shed with its collection of steam and diesel locomotives is open for the public to explore.

The **Lakeland Motor Museum** is about a mile away in the village of Backbarrow and is housed in a former watermill (www.lakelandmotormuseum.co.uk). The museum is dedicated to the history of motoring, with many classic cars, motorcycles, bicycles and scooters on display, and more unusual exhibits, such as pedal cars and caravans. However, there is much more to see, including recreations of historic street and garage scenes and exhibits on the Isle of Man TT races and the watermills and industrial history of the Leven valley.

The river is particularly dramatic here with rapids and whirlpools and there are good views from the museum's riverside café and from waterside paths nearby. Nearby sights include the remains of **Backbarrow Iron Works**, which operated until the 1960s (www.backbarrowironworks.org.uk), and Backbarrow Bridge, which is a picturesque historic arched bridge across the River Leven.

Haverthwaite to Roa Island

Heading west from Haverthwaite, the main coastal road crosses a marshy flood

Sunset view of the Ulverston Canal with the Sir John Barrow Monument in the distance (inset: Market Place, Ulverston)

plain alongside Rusland Pool, a small tributary of the Leven Estuary.

The first village on the western shores is Greenodd. This lies on the shores of the River Crake, which flows down from Coniston Water in the Lake District. A footpath crosses the Leven nearby giving access to the opposite shores.

Ulverston is a short way inland and was once a port, linked to the estuary by the Ulverston Canal. Nowadays the entrance to the canal is a tranquil spot with fine views of the estuary and the railway viaduct a short way upstream. The popular waterfront Bay Horse hotel and restaurant is nearby, and the disused pier is a good viewpoint for the Leven Tidal Bore, which is described later. This area can be reached by road past Ulverston's GlaxoSmithKline works or on foot along the canal towpath from the town.

Ulverston is a popular tourist destination with festivals throughout the year, including a Lantern Festival in September and the Dickensian Christmas Festival. There are many historic buildings along its cobbled streets and alleyways and a good choice of cafés and restaurants.

Other attractions include the **Sir John Barrow Monument**, described later, and the **Laurel and Hardy Museum**, established in honour of Stan Laurel who was born in the town (www.laurel-and-hardy.co.uk). Classic films starring the comedians are shown throughout the day and items on display include letters and photographs.

Heading further along the estuary, the coastal road passes **Conishead Priory**, now the home of the Manjushri Kadampa

▲ (Top to bottom) The pier at Canal Foot near Ulverston and the railway viaduct across the Leven Estuary; The Kadampa Buddhist Temple for World Peace at Conishead Priory (© Conishead Priory); Telephoto view from Birkrigg Common of Chapel Island and the Holy Trinity Church in Bardsea

Buddhist Centre and Temple. The Priory is an impressive restored country house, first completed in 1836 with ornate decorations in Romantic Gothic style. A medieval priory stood here before, until dissolved by Henry VIII. There are delightful woodland walks down to the estuary. Each afternoon the Kadampa Buddhist Temple is open to the public for meditation, and there is an active year-round programme of meditation courses and retreats. The popular café extends to an outdoor terrace and adjacent lawns (www.conisheadpriory.org).

Beyond the priory, the parking areas near **Bardsea** are a popular place to stop, with good views across the estuary. A small roadside café serves snacks and ice cream. In the village, Holy Trinity Church has a magnificent raised location and its spire is a distinctive landmark. On nearby Birkrigg Common, footpaths lead to prehistoric **Birkrigg Stone Circle**, one of several in Cumbria, as described in Chapter 1, Coastal themes.

Chapel Island is easily visible from the shore. Uninhabited, it is a refuge for wildlife. It was once an emergency refuge for travellers crossing the sands, although due to the risks from the tides

Birkrigg Stone Circle ▼

and quicksand, it must only be visited with an expert guide. Guided walks are sometimes organised by local charities and to Piel Island, further to the south, where there are similar dangers.

The Bardsea area marks the end of the Leven Estuary and the coastal road continues along the shores of Morecambe Bay toward Roa Island and the southerly end of the Furness Peninsula.

Barrow-in-Furness

Barrow-in-Furness is a short way beyond with its busy port and shipbuilding industry. It is the largest town around Morecambe Bay and has a similar population to the city of Lancaster.

The huge submarine fabrication sheds of BAE Systems are a distinctive feature, visible from miles away on a clear day. Much of the town was built in Victorian times and there are many grand buildings in the local sandstone, including the impressive town hall. The town's history is described at the **Dock Museum**, including exhibits on the Roman and Viking eras, social history and shipbuilding, with many intricate models made by shipyard workers.

The museum is built over a former dry dock and is situated close to the bridge to nearby Walney Island. There is a café and gift shop on site and nearby footpaths provide pleasant waterside walks to the bridge and along the coast. A fabulous interactive website gives a preview of exhibits at the museum and insights into the history of the Furness Peninsula from prehistoric times (www.dockmuseum.org.uk).

The islands near Barrow-in-Furness

Several islands lie near the tip of the Furness Peninsula and were formed at the end of the last Ice Age from the rocks and debris deposited by glaciers as they melted.

The largest is **Walney Island** and the shelter provided by its long, curving mass helps to make Barrow a natural port. Artificial causeways to Roa Island and Foulney Island provide further protection. Other notable islands include Piel Island and Sheep Island, while Barrow Island was a distinct island too before construction of the docks.

The causeway to **Roa Island** was built in the 19th century to carry a railway line to a steamship pier that once stood here. Nowadays, a much shorter pier leads to the RNLI Barrow Lifeboat Station, which is sometimes open to the public. This includes exhibits on the lifeboat service and a viewing gallery for the impressive all-weather lifeboat based here (www.rnli.org). Many yachts and leisure craft are based here too.

The popular Bosun's Locker Café is on the island. There are great views of nearby **Piel Island** and its main feature, **Piel Castle**. The castle was part of the **Furness Abbey** estate and the ruins include the remains of its impressive keep and inner and outer fortifications (www.english-heritage.org.uk). The grounds of the castle are open to explore although the inside is closed to visitors.

During the tourist season a motor launch ferries passengers to Piel Island, stopping at a pier in front of the Ship Inn, one of the few buildings on the island. The pub is popular with day-trippers

▲ The RNLI Barrow lifeboat station at Roa Island

Barrow waterfront seen from the bridge at Walney Island ▼

and offers camping accommodation. Since the 15th century, its landlords have had the honorary title of the King of Piel (www.pielisland.co.uk).

It is also possible to visit nearby **Foulney Island**, whose causeway is accessible on foot at low tide. However, it is essential to check tide tables first so as not to be stranded. The island is a Cumbria Wildlife Trust nature reserve (www.cumbriawildlifetrust.org.uk) and during the summer a warden lives on site to protect the birds that nest here; see later for more information. The causeway was built in the 19th century to help to reduce sedimentation in the approaches to Barrow's port.

As well as being the largest island, Walney Island extends the furthest from land. At its southern end it juts out into Morecambe Bay while the northern part lies in the Duddon Estuary. It is approximately ten miles long and just over a mile across at its widest point. The much smaller uninhabited Sheep Island lies off its shores.

The most populated area on the island is Vickerstown, which was built to house workers at Barrow's shipyards. The design included churches and a park. Billed as a 'marine garden city', conservation areas now preserve the architectural and historical character of this part of the town. The bridge that connects the island to the mainland was opened in 1908 to improve access for dock workers, and replaced a ferry service.

The nature reserves on the island are described later, but are best known for migratory waterbirds and a resident population of seals. In the northern part of the island, a former military airfield is now home to a gliding club, with occasional visits from larger aircraft in support of shipbuilding operations in Barrow.

Piel Island at low tide ▼

COASTAL VIEWPOINTS

When travelling around the Furness Peninsula, the open moorland roads afford some good views of the estuary, such as the area around Harlock Reservoir in the hills near Ulverston.

One of the best viewpoints is in Ulverston itself, in the form of the Sir John Barrow Monument. Resembling a lighthouse, it stands 30.5 metres tall and is situated on Hoad Hill (137m) just north of the town centre (www.ulverstoncouncil.org.uk).

▲ Humphrey Head and the Ulverston Canal seen from Hoad Hill in Ulverston

Built in 1850, it commemorates one of the town's most illustrious former residents, the 19th century explorer John Barrow, whose remarkable life is described later. The tower is open to the public on some summer weekends, with outstanding views of the estuary from the viewing gallery, which is reached by 112 steps. Other landmarks visible on a clear day include the Lake District fells, the Yorkshire Dales, Blackpool Tower and even north Wales. Plaques near the base of the tower show the distances and directions to key points. The surrounding park has pleasant walks and a café.

On the opposite shores of the estuary, opportunities to see it from on high are more limited due to the lack of access. However, for hillwalkers, the higher ground east of the B5278 is a possibility. Further south on the Cartmel Peninsula there are views of the coastal plain from some of the minor roads near the village of Allithwaite, with Barrow visible on a clear day.

Chapel Island and the Leven Estuary seen from hills inland from Ulverston ▼

The coastal plain seen from near Allithwaite

SOURCE TO SEA: RIVER LEVEN

The River Leven begins its journey to Morecambe Bay at the outlet from Windermere, England's largest natural lake. The waterside views and the Swan Hotel, with its outdoor terrace, make this a pleasant spot to visit.

The largest tributary of the lake is the River Rothay, which rises on slopes south of Helvellyn (950m), the third highest peak in the Lake District. It then flows through Grasmere, a picturesque lake with Grasmere village on its shores, and Rydal Water, before meeting Windermere in Ambleside.

Here it is joined by the River Brathay, which rises near Wrynose Pass. Its main tributary is Great Langdale Beck, which flows down from the Langdale Valley, surrounded by popular hillwalking peaks such as Bowfell (902m), Crinkle Crags (859m) and the spectacular jumble of peaks and crags of the Langdale Pikes. The shallow, marshy lake of Elterwater lies along its course.

On its western side, the Windermere catchment includes the beautiful artificial lake of Tarn Hows, a popular tourist destination, along with Esthwaite Water, which is the source of Cunsey Beck. On the opposite shores, Trout Beck flows into the lake between Ambleside and the town of Windermere, having risen in fells near to the Kirkstone Pass.

The outflows from Windermere are controlled by a weir at its outlet. The River Leven then passes through a winding valley, with a series of spectacular whirlpools and rapids in Backbarrow, before a more tranquil section leads to the start of the estuary near Haverthwaite.

A minor tributary, Rusland Pool, joins soon after and shortly downstream the River Crake flows into the estuary near the village of Greenodd. The Crake begins in Coniston Water, which is fed by runoff from the Coniston fells, where the high point is the Old Man of Coniston (803m).

Several smaller tributaries join further downstream, such as Dragley Beck, which passes through Ulverston, and Poaka Beck, once a source of water for Furness Abbey, which enters the estuary at Cavendish Dock in Barrow-in-Furness. Both have water supply reservoirs in their upper reaches.

The smaller Gleaston Beck rises in a picturesque glacier-carved lake called Urswick Tarn. Along with two nearby springs it once provided power to Gleaston watermill further downstream, which has been restored and is open to visitors (www.watermill.co.uk). The drainage patterns above the tarn are complex due to its limestone geology, and in part due to subsidence from iron ore mining in the 19th and 20th centuries.

On the opposite shoreline, the only significant inflow is from the River Eea, whose two main tributaries rise in a line of low hills just north of the Cartmel Peninsula. It then flows down through Cartmel and Cark to the estuary. Its unusual name is pronounced 'Ay' as in hay and may be derived from the Old Norse word for river.

(Inset Top) Yachts on Windermere ▶

(Inset Bottom) The River Leven at the outlet from Windemere with the Leven Estuary in the distance ▶

(Backdrop) A distant view of the Langdale Pikes ▶

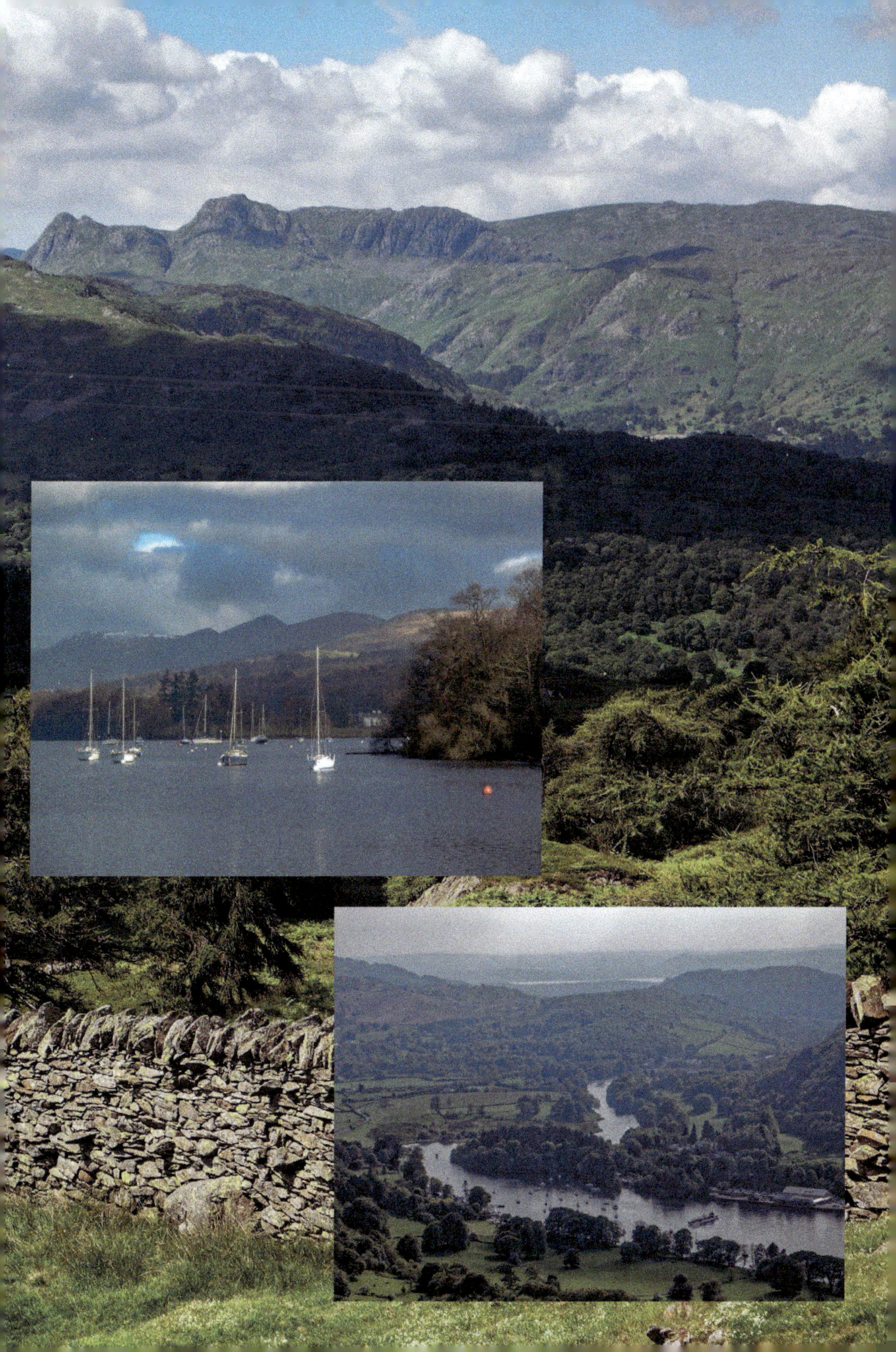

FURNESS ABBEY

Furness Abbey lies just north of Barrow and is one of the most impressive historic sites in Cumbria. Built in the local red sandstone, the abbey was established in the 12th century with land throughout south Cumbria. Its wealth and power was second only to that of Fountains Abbey in north Yorkshire. The main source of income was wool but iron ore and salt were important too. Iron was smelted using charcoal-fired pits and chimneys known as bloomeries.

Piel Castle, on an island off the coast, was one of its properties, helping to guard the entrance to a harbour on Walney Island. It also acted as a fortified store for products due for shipping, such as grain, wine, wool and pig iron. Nowadays it can be reached by ferry from Roa Island. The judicial centre and courts were in the market town of Dalton-in-Furness in a pele tower called Dalton Castle which is also open to visitors (www.nationaltrust.org.uk).

The abbey surrendered in 1537 under the Dissolution of the Monasteries and was the first large abbey to be destroyed. Features still standing include the remains of the church tower, the chapter house, the cloister buildings, the presbytery and the water supply and drainage system.

▲ Furness Abbey

The visitor centre has a museum and guide books are available (www.english-heritage.org.uk). During conservation work on the presbytery in 2010 the skeleton of an abbot was found and his crosier and a ring are on display. The Cistercian Trail passes alongside the grounds. This long-distance footpath extends to Grange-over-Sands via Cartmel Priory, another famous monastery in the region, which is described in the section on the Kent Estuary.

If visiting Dalton, the modern-day attraction of the South Lakes Safari Zoo is just a short distance away (www.southlakessafarizoo.com).

MORECAMBE BAY | 105

Maritime History

The Leven Estuary has long been used for fishing and coastal trade. Viking remains have been found, with some on display at the Dock Museum in Barrow-in-Furness (www.dockmuseum.org.uk), but there is little evidence that the Romans settled here, as they did further north in Cumbria. In medieval times, Piel Castle was an important outpost of Furness Abbey, as described opposite.

During the early stages of the industrial revolution, wharves and quays sprang up around the estuary to support local industries and sites included:

- Haverthwaite: a quay associated with the Low Wood Gunpowder Works and for shipments of iron ore to Backbarrow Iron Works, further up the River Leven
- Cark: wharves on the River Eea to support watermills producing paper, corn, hemp and other goods, and a small shipbuilding industry
- Bardsea and Conishead Bank: collection points for iron ore mined on the Furness Peninsula

Perhaps surprisingly, given its upstream location, Greenodd became the busiest port of all. Here several quays were built in the tidal reaches of the River Crake as far as Penny Bridge and ships were built here too. The goods handled included locally mined slate, limestone, copper and iron ore, and gunpowder made at the nearby Backbarrow works. Remarkably, there was even a daily steamship service to Liverpool.

Once the Furness Railway was built, the viaduct across the estuary limited access, although initially it included a drawbridge to allow ships to pass. Trade therefore shifted further downstream and the two main ports became Ulverston and Barrow.

At Ulverston, to help to avoid the vagaries of the tides, a canal was built from the town to the shoreline just over a mile away. Called the Ulverston Canal, this was one of the shortest waterways in the country. Ships would enter the canal through lock gates at Canal Foot and were then towed by horse to unload cargo at a dock basin and wharves in the town.

The canal was opened in 1796 and boosted trade in locally produced goods, such as bobbins, charcoal,

Telephoto view of Piel Castle from Walney Island ▼

The River Crake where it meets the Leven Estuary near Greenodd ▼

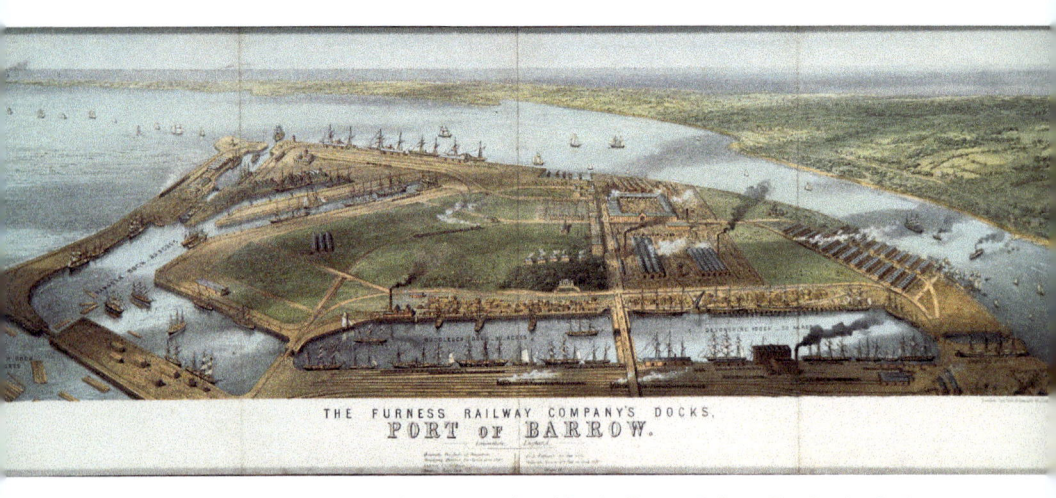

▲ Framed illustration of the Port of Barrow produced for the Furness Railway. The Graving Dock, Cavendish Dock, Buccleuch Dock and Ramsden Dock are shown, which dates the plan to circa 1880 (© The Dock Museum)

gunpowder, slate, and iron and copper ore. Destinations included Glasgow, Liverpool, Preston and Cardiff; cotton, coal and timber were traded in return. At its peak almost a thousand ships used the canal in a single year and a steamship passenger service operated from a pier at Canal Foot to Liverpool via Blackpool. Ships were built in the town until the late 19th century.

However, from the mid-19th century, trade began to decline due to competition from the railways and the growth of Barrow as a port. The last commercial use was in 1916 and the entrance gates were concreted up in 1949.

One of the first major developments in the Barrow area was the construction of a pier at Roa Island. This was later extended several hundred feet out toward the deeper water of Piel Channel, allowing ships to berth even at low tide. A railway station provided train connections for steamships bringing holidaymakers from Fleetwood and for ferry services to the Isle of Man and Belfast. These services ended once better facilities became available at Barrow.

The construction of the docks at Barrow began in the mid-19th century following the discovery of rich iron ore deposits on the Furness Peninsula. Until then Barrow had been a quiet fishing village with just a few quays for commercial traffic. Although not immediately obvious, the tip of the peninsula was once an island – Barrow Island – and the docks were created along the channel that separated it from the Furness Peninsula and by building retaining walls out to sea.

In little more than forty years, the town was transformed from a mainly farming and fishing village to become one of the largest iron-smelting and steelmaking centres in the world.

PLACES TO VISIT AROUND THE PORT OF BARROW

LIGHTHOUSES

Lighthouses were once essential for navigation and still have a valuable role to play. The first to be built in the area was for the Port of Lancaster, which in the 18th century was the largest port around Morecambe Bay.

This was Walney Lighthouse on the southern end of Walney Island and the original timber structure began operation in 1790. It was replaced with a stone structure in 1803 and in 2003 became the last lighthouse to be automated in the UK. It is now a key navigation aid for all shipping around Morecambe Bay.

▲ Walney Lighthouse

During the 19th century more than ten navigation beacons were built in the Barrow area to help guide ships to port. One still remains close to Roa Island and consists of a narrow square-section brick tower with a pyramid-shaped top, resembling a needle. This is called Rampside Lighthouse and is now a listed building.

CAVENDISH DOCK

Cavendish Dock was once part of the dock system at Barrow, connected to the other three docks but without a sea entrance. Its waters were enclosed by a sea wall alone, rather than by making use of the channel that connected Barrow Island to the mainland.

It was never fully completed as its opening in 1879 coincided with the start of a downturn in the iron ore trade. However, other uses were found over the years, including for a floating airship construction hanger, a floating store for a local timber yard, and a rope-making business.

In more recent times, it provided cooling water to nearby Roosecote Power Station. The water was then returned to the dock, making it slightly warmer than it would be otherwise. Levels were controlled by a sluice, at times allowing sea water in, and this combination of heat and salinity – carefully controlled – made the dock a haven for wildlife and freshwater fish, such as carp.

▲ View towards Barrow across Cavendish Dock

Nowadays, the dock remains important for wildlife and the footpath along the sea wall provides great views across the surrounding area. Along with Hodbarrow Lagoon on the Duddon Estuary, it is one of the more unusual habitats around the Cumbrian coastline.

SIR JOHN BARROW

The Sir John Barrow Monument in Ulverston is one of the most impressive places to visit around the Leven Estuary. Situated on Hoad Hill, and also known as the Hoad Monument, it was built in 1850 in honour of Sir John Barrow, who was born in the town. The design was modelled on the Eddystone Lighthouse near Plymouth.

John Barrow was born in 1764 and after clerical work in Liverpool joined a whaling expedition to Greenland, aged sixteen.

He became Second Secretary to the Admiralty in 1804, after teaching mathematics in London and postings to China and South Africa, and held that post for more than forty years. In that role he actively promoted exploration of new routes, particularly to west Africa and the search for a northwest passage around Canada.

He was fluent in Chinese and a founder member of the Royal Geographical Society. As a writer, his accounts of travels in China, Africa and the Arctic remain a valuable record of that period, as is his account of the Mutiny on the Bounty. The website of Ulverston Town Council gives more information on his achievements (www.ulverstoncouncil.org.uk).

The Sir John Barrow Monument ▼

THE LEVEN TIDAL BORE

The Leven Estuary is one of four around Morecambe Bay on which a tidal bore forms on the highest tides, the others being the Kent, Lune and Wyre estuaries.

From the shore it can first be seen downstream from Ulverston. It then travels upstream toward the railway viaduct across the Leven, sometimes crowned by a line of surf.

Perhaps the best viewpoint is from the old pier at Canal Foot near Ulverston. A low wave sometimes makes it almost as far as the confluence with the River Crake, for which one viewpoint is the car parking area near Greenodd. However, the river channel often changes course in this part of the estuary so the tidal bore may not get this far in some years, even in the best conditions.

As with all tidal bores, predicting its arrival is not an exact science and Chapter 1, Coastal themes, describes the typical conditions in which one forms. There is also background on why tidal bores occur and where to find out tide times.

The Leven Tidal Bore viewed from near the pier at Canal Foot ▶▼

The ready availability of steel led to a shipbuilding industry, and naval vessels became a speciality, particularly submarines. Other vessel types included steamships, barges, container ships and cruise liners. Steamship services to Fleetwood operated until the First World War.

Steelmaking ended in the 1980s but Barrow remains a busy port and shipbuilding centre; nowadays most of the Royal Navy's nuclear submarines are built here. Support services for wind energy are a more recent development, with one of the world's largest offshore wind farms about twelve miles from Walney Island.

A footpath around the now disused Cavendish Dock provides the chance to see vessels in port. Along the way, interpretation panels describe the local history and wildlife. The Dock Museum in Barrow is a great place to learn more about the history of the port. Heading north out of the town, a reminder of the past is a landscaped slag heap formed from the waste products of blast furnaces at what was once one of the largest ironworks in the world.

Wildlife

Like the other estuaries around Morecambe Bay, the Leven Estuary is famed for its wading birds, which in winter gather in large numbers on the mudflats and sandbanks exposed at low tide.

Heading inland from Humphrey Head, the eastern shores of the estuary are fringed by saltmarsh and sandbanks, while near the head of the estuary are remnants of the lowland raised mires that were once a feature of these shores. To the west, saltmarsh and sandbanks again become key features.

Both salmon and sea trout are found in its larger tributaries, and shrimp are caught in the estuary. In recent years, bristle strips have been installed at the outlet from Windermere to allow elvers (juvenile eels) to reach the lake as they migrate upstream.

Perhaps the most unusual habitat is beyond the estuary, in the intertidal areas around Barrow, where large expanses of saltmarsh, mud, sand and shingle are exposed at low tide, all in sight of the busy docks and shipping lane. Here the shelter provided by the islands has helped the saltmarsh to thrive. At low tide, extensive mussel beds attract species such as oystercatchers.

There are several nature reserves around the Leven Estuary and Furness Peninsula and the following sections

Seal pup at the South Walney Nature Reserve (© The Cumbria Wildlife Trust) ▼

describe perhaps the best known, at Walney Island, Foulney Island and Roudsea Woods.

Walney Island

Walney Island features two spectacular nature reserves, on the southern and northern tips of the island, looking out across Morecambe Bay and the Duddon Estuary.

At the southern end, South Walney Nature Reserve is an area of sand dunes, remote beaches, shingle bars and coastal vegetation where facilities include a visitor centre and several bird hides (www.cumbriawildlifetrust.org.uk).

More than 250 species of bird have been recorded here. The reserve is renowned as a nesting ground for eider ducks, little terns, and herring and lesser black-backed gulls, as well as the large numbers of wading birds that gather here in winter. Inland lagoons formed by sand and gravel extraction are another good place for birdwatching, and since the 1980s have been used by an oyster farm, whose products are exported worldwide. Spectacular dunlin and knot murmurations sometimes occur at the shoreline, as described in Chapter 1, Coastal themes.

However, it is grey seals that many visitors hope to see, and there is a resident population of several hundred, with several pups born each year. At low tide, seals tend to haul themselves out on a shingle spit at the end of the island, which is out of bounds, so binoculars or a telescope are required for the best views. For a closer look, a webcam

Shingle beach and mudflats at Foulney Island ▼

streams images to the visitor centre and to the Trust's website. On high tides seals sometimes swim close to the shoreline, particularly in a narrow inlet in sight of two of the bird hides.

Other highlights at the reserve include great views inland of distant fells, coastal walks, and Walney Lighthouse near the southern end, which as noted earlier plays a key role in navigation in Morecambe Bay. Workshops and guided walks are held throughout the year although it is important to check tide tables before visiting as access can be cut off on the highest tides.

At the opposite end of the island, North Walney National Nature Reserve is also important as a conservation area, although it has fewer facilities (www.gov.uk). The habitat includes sand dunes, dune heath, saltmarsh and shingle beaches. Insects and wildflowers are attracted to more sheltered areas. In winter, migratory birds that feed on the saltmarsh and mudflats include dunlins, redshanks and bar-tailed godwits. There is also a small population of rare natterjack toads. The reserve is managed by Natural England and only accessible on foot, with a choice of waymarked trails such as from parking areas near Earnse Point.

Foulney Island

Foulney Island lies at the southern end of the Furness Peninsula. Once a true island, since the late 19th century it has been connected to Roa Island by an artificial causeway. This was constructed to help to prevent the build-up of sediment in the channel which leads to the port at Barrow.

The island was formed from rocks and pebbles deposited by glaciers at the end of the last Ice Age. The shingle is favoured by nesting terns, and in the summer large numbers breed there, including arctic and little terns. Eider ducks, oystercatchers and several other species nest in the grassland and pebbles, while in winter the reserve is a haven for migratory wading birds.

The reserve is managed by Cumbria

Telephoto view of cormorants, eider ducks and oystercatchers at South Walney Nature Reserve ▼

▲ The upper reaches of the Leven Estuary, with Roudsea Wood and Mosses to the right of the image

▲ The road bridge over the River Leven near Low Wood

Wildlife Trust and there is a resident warden in summer to manage the site. The island is only accessible on foot and great care is needed not to get stranded since the causeway can be cut off by the tides for several hours. It is therefore essential to check tide tables first (www.cumbriawildlifetrust.org.uk). There are great views of Piel Island and the estuary along the way.

Roudsea Wood and Mosses

The Roudsea Wood and Mosses National Nature Reserve lies near the top of the estuary and includes an extraordinarily diverse range of habitats.

The reserve extends from the saltmarsh on the shores of the estuary to an extensive area of peat bog to the east of the woods. The mosses are some of the best-preserved in Cumbria, and plant species include cotton grass and sundews, as well as sphagnum mosses.

The underlying geology varies from slate to limestone, supporting a wide range of tree species. The transition zones between woods, mosses and saltmarsh support additional plant and insect species. More than fifty bird species have been recorded here and red squirrels and otters have been sighted too.

During the industrial revolution the woods were managed to provide charcoal for the nearby Low Wood Gunpowder Works. Nowadays they are still privately owned but leased to Natural England, who have established a network of trails through the reserve.

A permit is required to visit and details are available in an excellent brochure available on the Natural England website (www.naturalengland.org.uk).

A view toward Ravenglass

Chapter 3

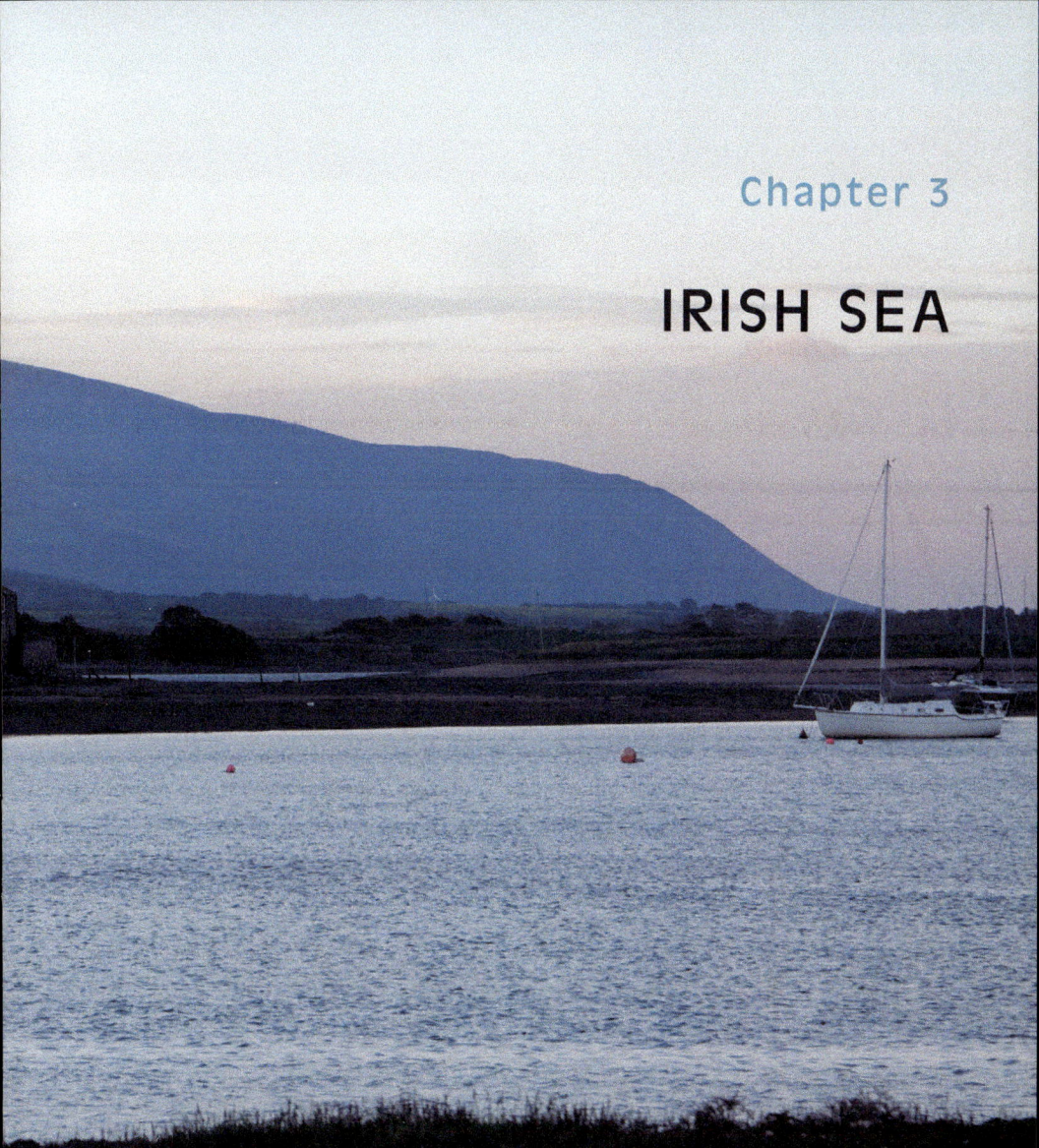

IRISH SEA

St Bees Head
St Bees
Pow Beck
River Ehen
Egremont
Ennerdale Water
River Liza
River Calder
Sellafield
Wastwater
Seascale
River Irt
River Mite
River Esk
Dalegarth
Ravenglass and Eskdale Railway
Muncaster Castle
Ravenglass
Irish Sea
Drigg Dunes
Ravenglass Estuary
Eskmeals Dunes
River Duddon
Kirkby Pool
Black Combe
Bootle
River Annas
Duddon Iron Furnace
Broughton-in-Furness
Duddon Mosses
Kirkby-in-Furness
Silecroft
Borwick Rails
Dunnerholme
Millom
Hodbarrow
Askam-in-Furness
Haverigg Point
Haverigg
Sandscale Haws
Duddon Estuary
North Walney
Furness Peninsula
Barrow-in-Furness
0
10
20 km
Railway
Motorway
Major road
Walney Island
Maps are indicative only. Contain
Ordnance Survey data © Crow
copyright and database right 202

▲ Irish Sea coast viewed from Black Combe; the view extends from Eskmeals Dunes across the Ravenglass Estuary to St Bees Head

The Irish Sea stretches from Pembrokeshire to southwest Scotland and in Cumbria meets the coast between Morecambe Bay and the Solway Firth.

Depths reach more than 200 metres to the west with a shallow coastal shelf along the Cumbrian coastline. Leatherback turtles and basking sharks are sighted occasionally, and seals, dolphins and porpoises too. The skeleton of a fin whale that was stranded on these shores is now on display at the Tullie House Museum & Art Gallery in Carlisle.

Along the Cumbrian coast, sand and shingle beaches are backed by sand dunes and low cliffs in places and several minor rivers meet the sea along its shores.

Highlights include seaside resorts and the historic town of St Bees, with its 12th century priory and a popular beach at the foot of dramatic sandstone cliffs.

The Duddon Estuary lies to the south and includes nature reserves, a historic iron furnace and other reminders of its industrial past. Further north, places to visit around the Ravenglass Estuary include a stately home, nature reserves and some of the best-preserved Roman ruins in Cumbria.

The beach and pier at Seascale with St Bees Head in the distance

IRISH SEA COAST

FEATURED LISTINGS

Bird's eye views	Black Combe
Historic buildings	St Bees Priory
Waterside walks	Irish Sea coast
Seaside visits	Silecroft
	Seascale
	St Bees

THE CUMBRIA AND LAKE DISTRICT COAST

> **INTRODUCTION**
> The Irish Sea coast is one of the least visited areas in Cumbria, but features sandy beaches and fine coastal views. Seaside destinations include Silecroft, Seascale and St Bees, with its historic priory.
>
> Several rivers meet these shores, including the Annan, Ehen and Pow Beck. Nearby attractions include the historic town of Egremont and one of the Lake District's finest valleys, Ennerdale, at the source of the Ehen.
>
> Its two main estuaries, the Duddon Estuary and Ravenglass Estuary, are described later in this chapter.

Places of interest

Heading north from the Duddon Estuary, the sand and shingle beach is initially backed by sand dunes. The beach at Silecroft is a popular spot for visitors, with a beach café and fine coastal views.

The first significant inflow is from the River Annas, which starts near the village of Bootle. Its headwaters are on the slopes of Black Combe and Corney Fell. **Black Combe** (600m) is the highest peak in this part of Cumbria and dominates the skyline. It is a great viewpoint for the Duddon Estuary and on a clear day views extend north beyond the Annas to the Ravenglass Estuary and St Bees Head.

On reaching the coast, the path of the river is blocked by a shingle bar formed by longshore drift, arising from deposition due to coastal currents. The outlet to the sea is about half a mile further north. Other shingle bars along the Cumbrian coastline include those at the mouths of the River Ehen and the

▲ (Top to bottom) The beach at Silecroft; Egremont Castle; The cliffs of St Bees Head seen from Seamill Foreshore

Ravenglass Estuary, and at Grune Point near Silloth on the Solway Firth.

The next major landmark is the military base of Eskmeals. The entrance to the Ravenglass Estuary lies to the north, fringed by sand dunes and nature reserves on both sides. Low cliffs then reappear before reaching the town of **Seascale**. This began as a Victorian holiday resort and its wooden jetty was restored as part of the Millennium celebrations. The miles of sandy beaches attract local residents and visitors alike.

The Sellafield nuclear engineering site lies shortly beyond. The River Ehen meets the coast here, having started at Ennerdale Water, one of the most beautiful lakes in the Lake District.

Ennerdale is a popular spot for hillwalkers and wildlife enthusiasts and is the site of Cumbria's largest rewilding project, as described in Chapter 1, Coastal themes. The upper reaches of the valley are surrounded by a string of well-known Lake District fells, including Great Gable (899m) and Pillar (892m).

Downstream from Cleator, the Ehen is joined by its largest tributary, the River Keekle. **Keekle Community Park** lies nearby and features waterside walks and an impressive railway viaduct. The Ehen then passes through the historic town of **Egremont**, overlooked by the ruins of 12th century Egremont Castle. The annual Egremont Crab Fair draws many visitors, and unusually for a traditional country fair includes the World Gurning Championships, during which participants compete to pull the most grotesque faces.

Approaching the coast, the Ehen turns southward after the village of Beckermet to cross a wide marshy floodplain alongside a shingle bar. It then passes beneath the coastal railway line to reach the sea. Within metres of the beach, it is joined by the smaller River Calder, which also rises in the Ennerdale area, and passes through the Sellafield site en route to the sea.

▲ St Bees Priory

The combination of sand, shingle and low cliffs then resumes, ending at the historic village of **St Bees**. Here, 12th century **St Bees Priory** is fascinating to visit, and the sandy beach, promenade and cafés are popular with holidaymakers. The long-distance Coast to Coast Path begins here, which passes through the Lake District, Yorkshire Dales and North York Moors to end at Robin Hood's Bay on the North Yorkshire coast.

Pow Beck meets the coast here. It rises in nearby coastal hills and in St Bees enters a steep valley before crossing the beach in a narrow channel. This area is called the Seamill Foreshore and is named after a grain mill that once stood nearby. It lies within sight of the spectacular sandstone cliffs of St Bees Head, a nesting ground for guillemots and even the occasional puffin. The RSPB reserve on the cliffs is discussed in Chapter 4, Solway Firth.

The Duddon Estuary viewed from hills near Kirkby-in-Furness

DUDDON ESTUARY

FEATURED LISTINGS

Bird's eye views	Dunnerholme
	Black Combe
Museums	Millom Heritage & Arts Centre
Maritime connections	Hodbarrow Lighthouse
Wildlife	Hodbarrow
Historic buildings	Duddon Iron Furnace
Ancient sites	Swinside Stone Circle
Waterside walks	Hodbarrow
Seaside visits	Haverigg
Tidal bore viewpoints	Dunnerholme

THE CUMBRIA AND LAKE DISTRICT COAST

INTRODUCTION

The Duddon Estuary lies at the southwestern tip of Cumbria, giving it a more remote and wild feel than some other locations around the coastline.

It is also one of the few places where the Cumbrian fells reach close to the shoreline, giving spectacular waterside views with a backdrop of Lakeland fells.

On its southeastern side, the estuary ends at Walney Island. Towns and villages along its shores include Askam-in-Furness and Kirkby-in-Furness, and the historic market town of Broughton-in-Furness is just a short distance inland.

The largest town is Millom, which was once an important iron-ore mining centre. The lagoon on the former mines at Hodbarrow is now part of a nature reserve famed for its bird life.

The attractive seaside village of Haverigg lies just beyond, with a wide sandy beach and a picturesque small harbour.

▲ (Top) Swans on Kirkby Pool and distant Lake District fells; (Bottom) The village of Foxfield, close to the railway viaduct over the estuary

Places of interest

Barrow-in-Furness to Broughton-in-Furness

The Duddon Estuary is flanked by the Furness Peninsula and the stocky mass of **Black Combe** (600m) on the opposite shores, one of the best coastal viewpoints in the region.

On its southeastern shores, the estuary ends at Walney Island, which is discussed in Chapter 2, Morecambe Bay. The Duddon's largest nature reserve, Sandscale Haws, is just across the water, north of Barrow-in-Furness. It is an area of sand dunes which is a haven for rare plants, insects and migrating waterbirds.

Heading inland, the main towns are Askam-in-Furness and Kirkby-in-Furness, whose origins lie in iron and slate mining. Highlights include waterside walks and estuary views.

Dunnerholme lies in between and is an impressive limestone promontory giving spectacular views inland of the Lake District fells and toward Black Combe. Perhaps surprisingly, it includes the putting green for the sixth hole of a nearby golf course.

The coastal railway crosses the estuary beyond Kirkby via an impressive

▲ Telephoto view of Dunnerholme

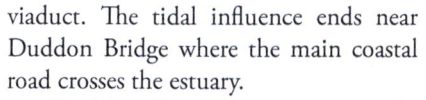

▲ Boats at Haverigg with Black Combe in the distance

viaduct. The tidal influence ends near Duddon Bridge where the main coastal road crosses the estuary.

Duddon Iron Furnace is on the banks of the river upstream of the bridge and has been restored by English Heritage. The picturesque historic town of **Broughton-in-Furness** is nearby, with a cobbled Georgian main square and traditional shops, pubs and cafés.

Broughton-in-Furness to Millom

Along the opposite side of the estuary, the shore is flanked by mudflats and saltmarsh, attracting huge numbers of wading birds in winter. Again, Black Combe dominates the skyline and **Swinside Stone Circle** lies high on its slopes. This is one of about fifty stone circles in Cumbria, as described in Chapter 1, Coastal themes. The 55 stones are on private land and visible from a nearby footpath.

An earth embankment protects areas inland from flooding on much of this side of the estuary. Access to these shores is limited, but from Green Road Station the last three miles or so of the embankment into Millom gives spectacular views across the estuary and inland to distant hills.

Millom is the largest town around the estuary and the pointed spire of St George's Church is a distinctive landmark for miles around. The former mine workings to the south were flooded to create Hodbarrow Lagoon, which is now within a RSPB nature reserve.

A short way beyond, the village of **Haverigg** lies at the mouth of Haverigg Pool. The smattering of leisure craft and fishing boats here makes for scenic photographs. With extensive areas of sand backed by sand dunes, it is a popular spot for sunbathing and waterside walks. The estuary ends a short way beyond at Haverigg Point.

Millom

Millom lies close to the mouth of the estuary and in medieval times a castle stood here. Its remains are on private land but are visible from nearby Holy Trinity Church.

Following the discovery of iron-ore deposits, Millom was established as a new town in the 1860s to accommodate the influx of workers to the mines and smelting works. St George's Church with its distinctive spire was built soon after.

The mine shafts were close to Hodbarrow Point to the south and continued out beneath the sea bed. In the late 1800s attempts were made to protect the mines from sand and water incursions by building sea walls; the current wall – the Outer Barrier – was completed in 1905 and remains to this day. It is a remarkable structure, extending the shoreline out to sea between Haverigg and Hodbarrow Point, and pumps and a sluice once helped to keep the mines drained. The works were closed in the 1960s, leading to a change in the town's fortunes.

This industrial past is described at **Millom Heritage & Arts Centre**, along with the social, maritime and cultural history of the town. Exhibits include a full-scale mock-up of a mine cage used to transport miners down the pit shafts and samples of locally mined ore. Other displays include reminders of the former

▲ (Top to bottom) St George's Church in Millom viewed across Hodbarrow Lagoon; The Outer Barrier and lighthouse at Hodbarrow; Former mine workings near Hodbarrow

COASTAL VIEWPOINTS

There are several great places to see the Duddon Estuary from on high, starting with the hills of the Furness Peninsula. If cycling or driving, perhaps the most accessible viewpoint is from the parking areas along the road from the moors to Kirkby-in-Furness. Here the steep final section provides extensive views across the estuary to Black Combe.

The low promontory of Dunnerholme is another option. This too provides great views inland and toward Black Combe, and is accessible by footpaths from Askam-in-Furness. The route over the sands should be avoided though as the tide comes in fast here and the shoreline around the promontory is a known high-risk area for quicksand.

▲ View inland from Dunnerholme

Other great viewpoints include the sea wall at Hodbarrow and the sea defence embankment near Millom. Perhaps the finest of all though is Black Combe (600m), particularly from the slightly lower south summit, which is reached by a faint path from the top. On a clear day, the views extend to St Bees Head to the north and the Coniston fells further inland in the Lake District.

The ascent of Black Combe is a serious hill walk requiring appropriate clothing and footwear, map-reading skills and a good level of fitness. Route details appear in most walking guides to the Lake District.

▼ The Duddon Estuary and railway viaduct viewed from Black Combe

SOURCE TO SEA: RIVER DUDDON

The River Duddon rises near Wrynose Pass (393m), one of the highest road crossings in the Lake District, and has one of the most beautiful and remote valleys in the Lake District.

The pass is the site of the Three Shire Stone, which marks the former boundary of Lancashire with that of the historic counties of Cumberland and Westmorland, which existed until the 1970s.

After a steep initial section, the Duddon flows along a narrow gently sloping valley, flanked by fells on either side. The road from Wrynose Pass drops down to the valley floor too.

Cockley Beck joins the Duddon at a small hamlet of the same name. From here, the combined flows turn southwards toward the coast, initially passing over a flatter area, with fine views of the fells around.

Tarn Beck then joins from remote Seathwaite Tarn, which is the only sizeable body of water in the catchment and is part of the water supply system for Barrow-in-Furness. Beyond lies Wallowbarrow Gorge where the spectacular rapids and waterfalls are a popular playground for kayakers.

The valley widens again but remains steep, and the Duddon only reaches the coastal margins close to the top of the estuary, where it is joined by the River Lickle, to reach Duddon Bridge. The normal tidal limit is a short way downstream, although may extend further inland on the highest tides.

The only major river that flows into the estuary is Kirkby Pool, which joins the shoreline at Kirkby-in-Furness. A small estuary has formed at its outlet, which is a scenic spot as the river winds its way across saltmarsh, with great views of distant hills beyond.

The smaller Haverigg Pool flows into the estuary at Haverigg and rises on the slopes of Black Combe. Initially called Whicham Beck it flows along the narrow Whicham Valley before reaching the coastal plain. Black Beck also flows down from Black Combe and is smaller still, joining the estuary upstream from Millom.

▼ The upper reaches of the River Duddon from near Wrynose Pass

Birks Bridge upstream of Wallowbarrow Gorge; (Inset) Duddon Bridge

THE CUMBRIA AND LAKE DISTRICT COAST

RAF airfield at Millom and examples of prehistoric fossils and rocks from the area. The centre includes a shop and rail ticket office and is situated at the railway station (www.millomhac.co.uk).

After mining ended, the pits were allowed to flood to form an artificial lagoon. This area is now the centrepiece of the RSPB's **Hodbarrow Nature Reserve**, which is described later. In addition to wildlife watching it provides pleasant waterside and woodland walks, including spectacular views inland from the sea wall, which features a lighthouse and bird hides.

Quarrying continues at the nearby Ghyll Scaur Quarry, where crushed stone has been extracted for road building since the 1930s.

Maritime history

With a high tidal range and extensive shifting areas of sandbanks, the upper Duddon Estuary is challenging to navigate, so was not a natural site for a port.

However, in the deeper water downstream a coastal trade developed as the industrial revolution got underway, with a natural harbour at the unusually named site of Borwick Rails. This was close to the old village of Holborn Hill, which was absorbed into Millom when the new town was built in the mid-1800s. The goods handled included shipments of slate, coal and corn.

There was also trade from Haverigg a short way around the coast where Haverigg Pool provides a sheltered spot to anchor. Barges from Kirkby-in-Furness carried slate here and to Millom to be loaded onto larger vessels. In the 18th century there would have been shipping associated with the Duddon Iron Furnace with barges bringing iron ore from the Furness Peninsula for onward transport by horse and cart.

▼ Telephoto view of Hodbarrow Lighthouse from Dunnerholme

THE DUDDON TIDAL BORE

As in several other estuaries around Cumbria, a tidal bore sometimes forms in the Duddon Estuary on the highest tides. It is quite challenging to spot as it runs along channels offshore for much of its passage.

Perhaps the best viewpoint is from the spectacular Dunnerholme promontory near Askam-in-Furness. Initially, the bore appears as a distant line of surf on the far side of the estuary, sometimes along two distinct channels. These then merge to follow a winding path across the estuary toward the rock, dissipating in a deep pool nearby. Here it loses much of its energy in a maelstrom of swirling water, attesting to the power of the flow. On the highest tides it continues upstream in much weakened form as a low wave.

Access routes to Dunnerholme were discussed earlier and Chapter 1, Coastal themes, describes how tidal bores form and gives tips on water safety. This includes conditions for formation of the Duddon's tidal bore, although as with any natural phenomenon it does not always occur as expected.

▲ The Duddon Tidal Bore viewed from Dunnerholme ▼

132 | THE CUMBRIA AND LAKE DISTRICT COAST

▲ Duddon Iron Furnace

The need for safe anchorage increased dramatically with the discovery of iron ore at Hodbarrow and Askam in the 1860s. This led to a major expansion of the facilities at Borwick Rails and the building

▼ The old lighthouse at Hodbarrow

of a platform out into the estuary at Askam where ships could berth. This was constructed from discarded slag from the town's ironworks and is known as Askam Pier.

A pier was also built at Borwick Rails, which by the turn of the century could accommodate several steamships and sailing ships. A stone-built lighthouse was replaced with a cast-iron structure in 1905 when the new sea wall was built.

Within a few decades the mining industry started to decline. The mining company disposed of its shipping fleet after World War I and the lighthouse was last used in 1949.

To find out more about the shipping history of the town, Millom Heritage & Arts Centre is a great place to start.

Exhibits include photographs, model ships, and the figurehead from the prow of the *Emily Barratt*, a sailing ship that operated from Borwick Rails.

Other interesting places to visit include Hodbarrow Lighthouse and the remains of the older stone structure on a low hill nearby. Other signs of this maritime past include Askam Pier and the well-preserved buildings of Duddon Iron Furnace. Looking to the future, current developments at Port Millom are described at www.portmillom.co.uk.

Wildlife

The sands of the Duddon Estuary are important winter feeding grounds for wading birds; numbers regularly exceed twenty thousand, with many more in severe winters. Visitors include knots, pintails, redshanks, sanderlings, dunlins, curlews and ringed plovers.

Saltmarsh fringes much of the middle and upper estuary and is another valuable habitat, as are the sand dunes around the mouth of the estuary at Haverigg and Sandscale Haws. Formed from the waste products from blast furnaces, slag banks near Millom and Askam-in-Furness provide unusual breeding grounds for some species of waterbirds.

There are several nature reserves around the estuary, including the Hodbarrow reserve near Millom, Sandscale Haws reserve near Barrow-in-Furness, and Duddon Mosses reserve at the top of the estuary.

DUDDON IRON FURNACE
Duddon Iron Furnace was one of eight furnaces built in the early 18th century to produce pig iron on an industrial scale. This could be melted down to make iron products and was exported to south Wales, the Midlands and beyond to make ship chains, anchors and other nautical goods.

The furnace was powered by charcoal produced from the surrounding woodland and used locally mined iron ore from the Furness Peninsula and west Cumbria. Water diverted from the River Duddon was used to drive a waterwheel that powered the bellows to pump air into the furnace.

Now managed by the Lake District National Park Authority, the furnace is situated a short way upstream of Duddon Bridge (www.lakedistrict.gov.uk). The well-preserved remains include the charcoal and iron ore stores and the 29-foot-high chimney stack. The furnace was operated from 1736 to 1867.

Hodbarrow Nature Reserve

The Hodbarrow reserve was created in an area that was once the centre for mining activity near Millom. The centrepiece is the artificial lagoon formed when water was allowed to flood the former mine workings.

The main part of the reserve is to the east of the lagoon and pleasant walks through woods and grassland lead to the sea wall. From here there are fine views toward Millom and the mass of Black Combe, and of the lighthouse that once guided ships to port.

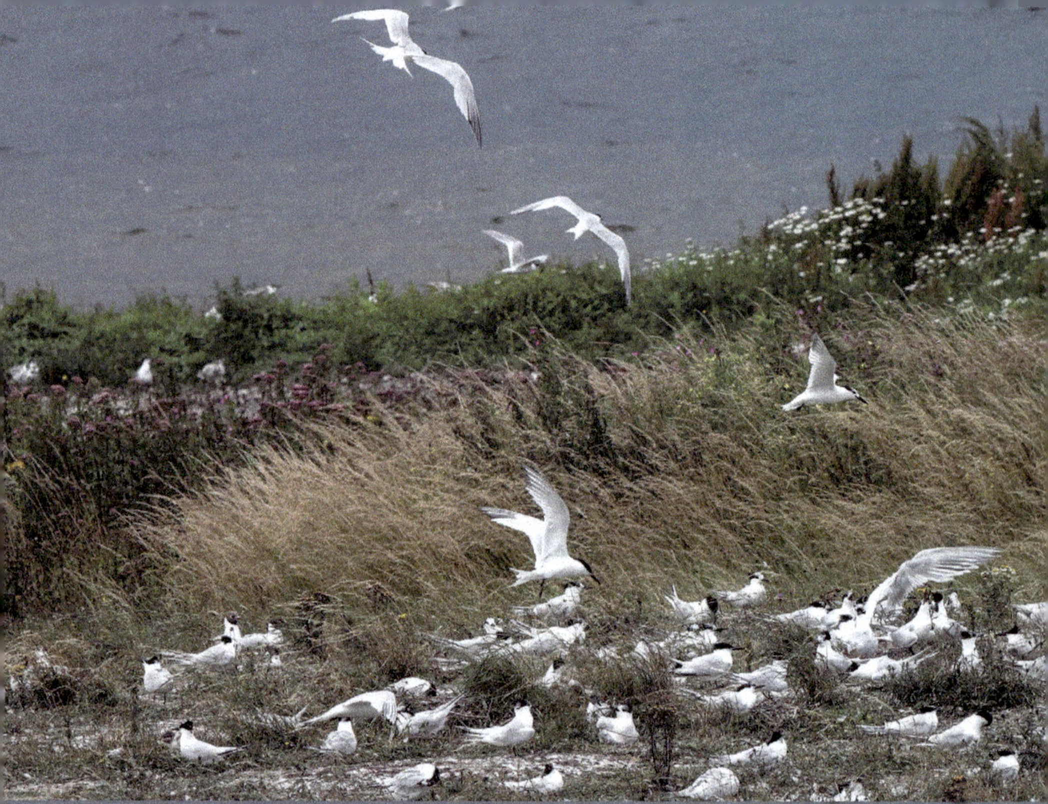
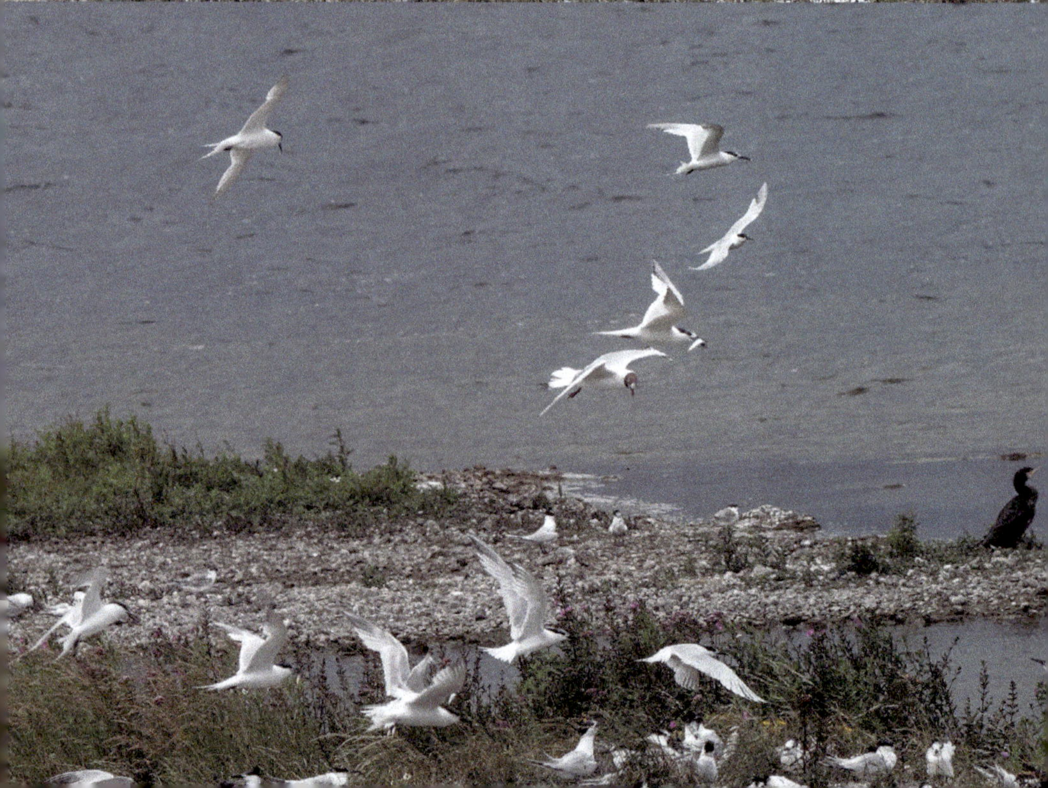

During winter, wading birds feed on the sands at low tide and grey seals are sometimes seen basking on sandbanks offshore.

Near the lighthouse, bird hides look out onto an island on the lagoon. This is a renowned breeding ground for the increasingly rare little tern. These migrate here from west Africa and in early summer several hundred can be seen nesting and making fishing trips for their favoured prey of sand eels and sprats.

Common and sandwich terns breed here too, as well as great crested grebes, lapwings, ringed plovers and oystercatchers. Several species of duck frequent the lagoon waters. In winter the island is a high tide roost for some species of wading birds, such as redshanks, lapwings and knots. The surrounding grasslands are a haven for songbirds and insects.

The reserve is managed by the RSPB (www.rspb.org.uk). The entrance is about 1.5 miles from Millom and is well signposted from the high street. A map at the entrance shows the main paths and bird hides. From the lighthouse the path along the sea wall continues to the picturesque village of Haverigg.

Although not part of the reserve, the Millom Ironworks Local Nature Reserve is nearby. This lies on the site of a former ironworks and in addition to birds and

◄ Terns and gulls at the RSPB Hodbarrow reserve with a cormorant in the lower photograph

Information board at Duddon Mosses National Nature Reserve ▼

insects shelters rare natterjack toads. The toads are difficult to spot, although the males make a loud mating call in spring and early summer.

Sandscale Haws National Nature Reserve

Sandscale Haws is an area of sand dunes near to the mouth of the Duddon Estuary with great views inland to the Lake District fells (www.nationaltrust.org.uk).

The sand dune grassland shelters a significant population of natterjack toads as well as lizards, butterflies and great crested newts.

Other highlights include wildflower displays in the spring and summer.

In winter huge numbers of wading birds feed on the mudflats at low tide, including redshanks, dunlins and sanderlings.

The reserve is about three miles north of Barrow-in-Furness. It lies just across the water from North Walney National Nature Reserve, which has a similar habitat and is described in Chapter 2, Morecambe Bay.

Duddon Mosses National Nature Reserve

The reserve at Duddon Mosses protects some of the remnants of the lowland raised peat bogs that once fringed the southern and northern shores of

Cumbria. Chapter 1, Coastal themes, describes how these formed.

The mosses are thought to have started accumulating several thousand years ago and are up to six metres deep. They are havens for insects and birdlife, and even the rare sundew, an insect-eating plant. Red deer and roe deer graze in the surrounding woodlands.

As at other similar reserves, areas of peat damaged due to extraction are being restored by blocking drains and removing scrub. Raised boardwalks allow visitors to explore the mosses along two circular walks (www.gov.uk). The mosses are in several parts and stretch north from near Foxfield toward the general area of Broughton-in-Furness. There is no car park but they can be reached on foot from either location.

Saltmarsh and sandbanks of the upper Duddon Estuary viewed from near Kirkby-in-Furness ▼

Ravenglass Estuary in early morning sunlight

RAVENGLASS ESTUARY

FEATURED LISTINGS

Bird's eye views	Newtown Knott
Museums	Ravenglass Railway Museum
Historic buildings	Muncaster Castle
Ancient sites	Roman Bath House
Waterside walks	Ravenglass

INTRODUCTION

On the west coast of Cumbria, three rivers flow into the Ravenglass Estuary from the Lake District fells. The main settlement is Ravenglass, an attractive coastal village.

Steam trains take visitors inland and forest walks lead to Muncaster Castle, a stately home with historic events throughout the year and bird of prey displays.

Sand dunes and beaches fringe the estuary mouth, making it a natural harbour. It has been used since Roman times and the ruins of a Roman bath house are some of the best preserved in the UK.

Large numbers of wading birds feed on the mudflats in winter and the sand dunes shelter bird-nesting sites and rare natterjack toads.

Places of interest

The Ravenglass Estuary lies on the Irish Sea coast and is the only estuary completely within the Lake District National Park. Unusually, it is at the outlet of three rivers, the Esk, the Irt and the Mite, which flow down from the Lakeland fells.

The outlet from the estuary lies between two lines of sand dunes. These are the centrepiece of the **Eskmeals Dunes** and **Drigg Dunes** nature reserves and are havens for nesting birds and rare natterjack toads.

The village of **Ravenglass** lies on the shores of the estuary. The wide main street is flanked by picturesque cottages, some dating back to the 18th century, and was once the site of a medieval

▲ (Top to bottom) Ravenglass viewed across the Esk; St Bees Head seen from the beach near Drigg Dunes

market. It leads to a slipway that provides easy access to the estuary, and the moored boats add to the atmosphere. There is a good mix of hotels and pubs.

The village is served by the mainline coastal railway. The station is also the terminus for the **Ravenglass & Eskdale Railway**, on which steam trains transport visitors into the Esk Valley. Highlights in the valley include riverside walks, traditional pubs, a restored watermill and spectacular views of some of the highest peaks in the Lake District.

Ravenglass was once the southern outpost of a line of Roman forts that stretched around the Cumbrian coastline from Hadrian's Wall on the Solway Firth. The **Roman Bath House** near the estuary shores is one of the best preserved in the country, and is about a mile from the village.

Another pleasant walk is to follow the shores of the estuary across a bridge over the River Mite. The path continues along the shoreline with fine views back inland.

Heading inland, there are many miles of footpaths in the forested hills behind Ravenglass. Some lead to the stately home of **Muncaster Castle**, which hosts events throughout the year and has a Hawk & Owl Centre. The formal gardens are a delight to visit and the terrace in front of the castle has spectacular views along the Esk Valley. There are also places to eat and gift shops (www.muncaster.co.uk).

The Ravenglass and Eskdale Railway

During the industrial revolution many valleys in the Lake District were hives of mining activity, with products including slate, granite, gypsum, copper and iron. The Esk Valley was no exception and in 1875 a narrow-gauge railway was built to transport iron ore from a mine near Dalegarth to Ravenglass for shipping to other destinations.

The railway wasn't a financial success and closed in 1913. It reopened two years later with a new track to serve a granite quarry, also carrying tourists in the summer. After struggling financially again, it was saved in 1960 with the formation

▲ (Top to bottom) A steam train travelling towards Ravenglass; 'The River Mite' locomotive crossing the River Esk near Dalegarth

of the Ravenglass & Eskdale Railway Preservation Society, soon becoming one of the Lake District's most popular tourist attractions.

The railway now carries more than 100,000 passengers a year, with a mix of open-air and covered seating (www.ravenglass-railway.co.uk). Of the six steam locomotives in use or under restoration, three are named after the rivers that flow into the Ravenglass Estuary.

Affectionately known as *La'al Ratty* – Old Cumbrian dialect for 'little rat track' – the line begins in Ravenglass and extends for seven miles to Dalegarth for Boot, a journey of about forty minutes. The main engine sheds and workshops in Ravenglass are open to visitors and the station has a café and gift shop. The popular Ratty Arms pub is alongside a nearby platform for the main coastal railway.

Dalegarth Station is just a few miles from the Lake District's highest peak, Scafell Pike (978m), and in addition to the valley views and a café, there is the unusual sight of locomotives being spun around on a turntable before making the return journey.

Some visitors explore further afield from Dalegarth or one of the seven intermediate request stops. Attractions include country pubs and hill and riverside walks. Another popular side trip is to Eskdale Mill, which has the last remaining working water-powered corn mill in the Lake District (www.eskdalemill.co.uk). It is a short walk from Dalegarth Station along a signposted route. Muncaster Mill, which still appears on some maps, is now a private residence, having once been open to visitors.

A handy guide can be downloaded from the railway's website with maps and ideas for places to visit. Services are seasonal although occasionally run at other times, such as around Christmas and Halloween.

Ravenglass Railway Museum nearby celebrates the history of the line including its granite and iron-ore mining past (www.ravenglassrailwaymuseum.co.uk). Items on display include locomotives, wagons, carriages and signalling equipment. Interactive displays describe how a steam engine works and the lives and times of people who worked on the railway. There is also a community exhibition area.

▼ Sand dunes at the Ravenglass Estuary

COASTAL VIEWPOINTS

The closest viewpoint for the estuary is Newtown Knott, which lies in the woods behind Ravenglass village. This can be reached by paths from Ravenglass or Muncaster Castle.

From here there are views of the rivers Irt and Esk and the outlet from the estuary, with the Eskmeals and Drigg dunes alongside.

Further afield perhaps the best views are from Black Combe (600m) where the Ravenglass Estuary is clearly visible in the distance on a fine day. This is also a great place to see the Duddon Estuary as described earlier.

The Ravenglass Estuary is also visible from the road that drops down from Corney Fell toward the coast, and from footpaths in the surrounding hills.

▲ The complex shape of the Ravenglass Estuary viewed from Corney Fell

▲ Eskmeals Dunes, Drigg Dunes and the mouth of the Ravenglass Estuary viewed from Newtown Knott

SOURCE TO SEA: THE RIVERS OF THE RAVENGLASS ESTUARY

Of the three rivers that flow into the estuary, the largest is the Esk. Its tributaries rise on the slopes of the highest mountain in the Lake District, Scafell Pike (978m), and it then descends steeply through a spectacular series of rapids and falls into the main valley.

Here the valley floor widens, flanked by hills on both sides, with some beautiful woodland and riverside walks. Stanley Ghyll Force is one of the most impressive waterfalls in the Lake District and lies on a tributary of the Esk. As noted earlier, the restored Eskdale Mill is a fine example of one of the many watermills once found along this valley. Other attractions include rural pubs and the Ravenglass & Eskdale Railway.

The Esk flows into the Ravenglass Estuary on its southern shores and the next largest river, the Irt, joins from the northeast. The Irt begins in Wast Water, a remote and beautiful lake in the west of the Lake District, which is on the opposite side of Scafell Pike to the Esk. This area is popular with hillwalkers and well-known surrounding peaks include Great Gable (899m) and Pillar (892m).

▲ The lowermost reaches of the River Esk before reaching the Ravenglass Estuary

The smallest river around the estuary is the Mite, and its headwaters are between those of the Esk and the Irt. It is fed by tributaries flowing down from Muncaster Fell (231m), a long, low ridge that climbs inland from the coastal plain. The Ravenglass & Eskdale Railway follows the Mite before crossing over into the Esk Valley beyond Muncaster Fell.

Due to the slope of the terrain, tidal influences only extend a short way inland on all three rivers. The usual tidal limits are close to the A595 coastal road on the Esk and near the railway bridges over the Mite and the Irt. In their lowermost reaches, mudflats and sandbanks are evident at low tide, with rushes and woodland on the surrounding floodplain.

There are no tidal bores, probably due to their steep slopes and because the tidal inflow is partly dissipated in the wide, shallow bay of the estuary.

The upper Esk Valley;
The headwaters of the
River Esk (inset)

Wasdale Screes at Wast Water; Wasdale viewed from the slopes of Great Gable (inset)

Maritime history

With a narrow entrance between sand dunes, the Ravenglass Estuary is a natural harbour and was probably an important port in Roman times.

Little is known of its history before the industrial revolution, but by the mid-1700s it was a busy port with a harbour master who collected anchorage fees on behalf of the Earl of Egremont.

In 1823 a beacon was built on Newtown Knott behind Ravenglass to help guide ships into port. It was kept whitewashed to make it more visible. Trade extended to Ireland, Scotland and the Isle of Man.

As local historian the Reverend Caesar Caine noted in the 19th century *The trade at this time consisted principally of corn, flour, oysters, oatmeal, bacon, iron, lime, potatoes, coal and various kinds of wood, such as spars, hoops, etc. Other than a wharf though, this remained a natural harbour, with no evidence of docks or piers.*

Lawson's Chart, a navigational chart from that era, suggested that to indicate the direction to the harbour the beacon should be lined up with another on the sand dunes south of the entrance. This was called a leading light approach and was a widely used navigational aid, such as at the entrance to the Lune Estuary in Morecambe Bay and the Port of Silloth on the Solway Firth.

As with many other ports and harbours around Cumbria, trade declined with the advent of the railways. Siltation of the rivers may also have played a role. The last cargo vessel that used the harbour was probably around the time of World War I.

The Roman Port

During Roman times, Ravenglass was the southernmost limit of a line of defences stretching around the coast from the end of Hadrian's Wall on the Solway Firth.

The main role of the naval base would have been to supply food, equipment and reinforcements via a Roman road to forts at Hardknott near the top of the Esk Valley and at Ambleside on the shores of Windermere. The western parts of Hadrian's Wall were probably supplied from Maryport to the north.

The fort in Ravenglass was known as Glannoventa and was situated on a low cliff overlooking the Esk. An artist's impression from a community excavation project suggests it was probably in the form of a walled compound containing barrack blocks, administrative buildings, the commander's residence and a central headquarters. It was surrounded by a sizeable civilian settlement or *vicus* that served the needs of the fort.

Finds of imported pottery suggest an active coastal trade, and the waste from iron smelting indicates that there were blacksmiths to make armour, tools and parts for boats. The fort may have been damaged and rebuilt several times before the Romans finally abandoned it early in the fifth century, after about 300 years.

Few signs of the fort remain, due to coastal erosion and because stones and other materials were reused in local buildings and to construct the coastal railway. However, the ruined walls of the

Leisure craft are the only boats seen near Ravenglass nowadays ▼

▲ The Roman Bath House at Ravenglass

bath house still stand and are now known as Walls Castle.

Standing about four metres high, it is one of the largest remaining Roman structures left in England, possibly because it remained in use as a house during medieval times. About half of the original structure remains. The site is about a mile's walk from Ravenglass Station along well-signed paths. Interpretation panels nearby describe the history of the Roman presence and a plan of the bath house suggests that it once had a changing room and warm rooms, a cold plunge and a hot bath.

Chapters 1 and 4 give more background on the Roman occupation in Cumbria, including other interesting places to visit such as the Senhouse Roman Museum, Milefortlet 21 and the Tullie House Museum & Art Gallery.

Wildlife

The Ravenglass Estuary flows out to the sea between two long lines of sand dunes, and in winter its mudflats are valuable feeding grounds for wading birds such as oystercatchers and curlews. The mudflats are most extensive at the mouths of the Irt and the Mite while the sediment deposited by the Esk has a higher sand content.

The hills behind the estuary are extensively forested and contain a wide variety of bird species, as well as a population of red squirrels. However, the only nature reserves are those that protect Eskmeals and Drigg dunes.

Oystercatchers with Ravenglass in the background ▼

Eskmeals Dunes Nature Reserve

The dunes at Drigg and Eskmeals were formed as sand accumulated on shingle bars that built up along the coastline, blocking the flow of the rivers to the sea.

Those to the south are part of the Eskmeals Dunes Nature Reserve, which is reached from a minor road off the A595 (www.cumbriawildlifetrust.org.uk). This is a Cumbria Wildlife Trust site and is leased from the Ministry of Defence, who operate the Eskmeals Range. The range is used for testing large calibre weapons, which are fired harmlessly out to sea. As the Trust's website states:

▲ A heron at Muncaster Castle

The public footpath leading to the reserve entrance can be very muddy and slippery. Please note the reserve is not accessible at

Drigg Dunes and Ravenglass viewed from the Eskmeals Dunes reserve ▼

high tide. IMPORTANT – If the yellow flag is flying, firing is taking place on the gun range and there is no access to the reserve. PLEASE RING THE GUN RANGE ON 01229 712200 BEFORE VISITING TO CHECK IF THE RESERVE IS OPEN.

The sand and shingle plus the saltmarsh alongside support a surprisingly large number of plant species, including wild thyme, sea lavender and glasswort. Several species of orchid grow in the dunes, including pyramidal, bee and northern marsh orchids.

Plant species vary with the terrain, with some preferring the sheltered valleys between dunes, while tougher marram grass grows in more exposed areas next to the coast. The tops of the dunes are a good viewpoint for Ravenglass and distant Lake District fells.

The plant life in turn attracts butterflies and insects such as dragonflies, while several natural and artificial ponds are breeding grounds for common and great crested newts, frogs and toads. This includes the rare natterjack toad. Woodland species such as stonechats, grey partridges and skylarks nest in the dunes.

Seasonal highlights include wildflowers in spring, nesting birds and butterflies in summer, and increasing numbers of migratory wading birds and wildfowl from autumn through to winter. Access roads are sometimes flooded at high tide and signs warn of the risks.

Drigg Dunes Local Nature Reserve

The dunes to the north of the estuary mouth support a similar variety of birdlife, plants and insects and are part of the Drigg Coast SSSI. This is one of the largest dune systems along the coast (www.naturalengland.org.uk).

Access is from the village of Drigg, where a surprising sight is the security fence of a low-level nuclear waste store which is associated with the Sellafield works to the north. A parking area lies shortly beyond.

There is a wide sandy beach along the coast, with great waterside walks with views toward Black Combe and the cliffs of St Bees.

Chapter 1, Coastal themes, gives more background on the habitat and wildlife of these and other sand dunes around the Cumbrian coastline.

Saltmarsh in the Solway Firth

Chapter 4

SOLWAY FIRTH

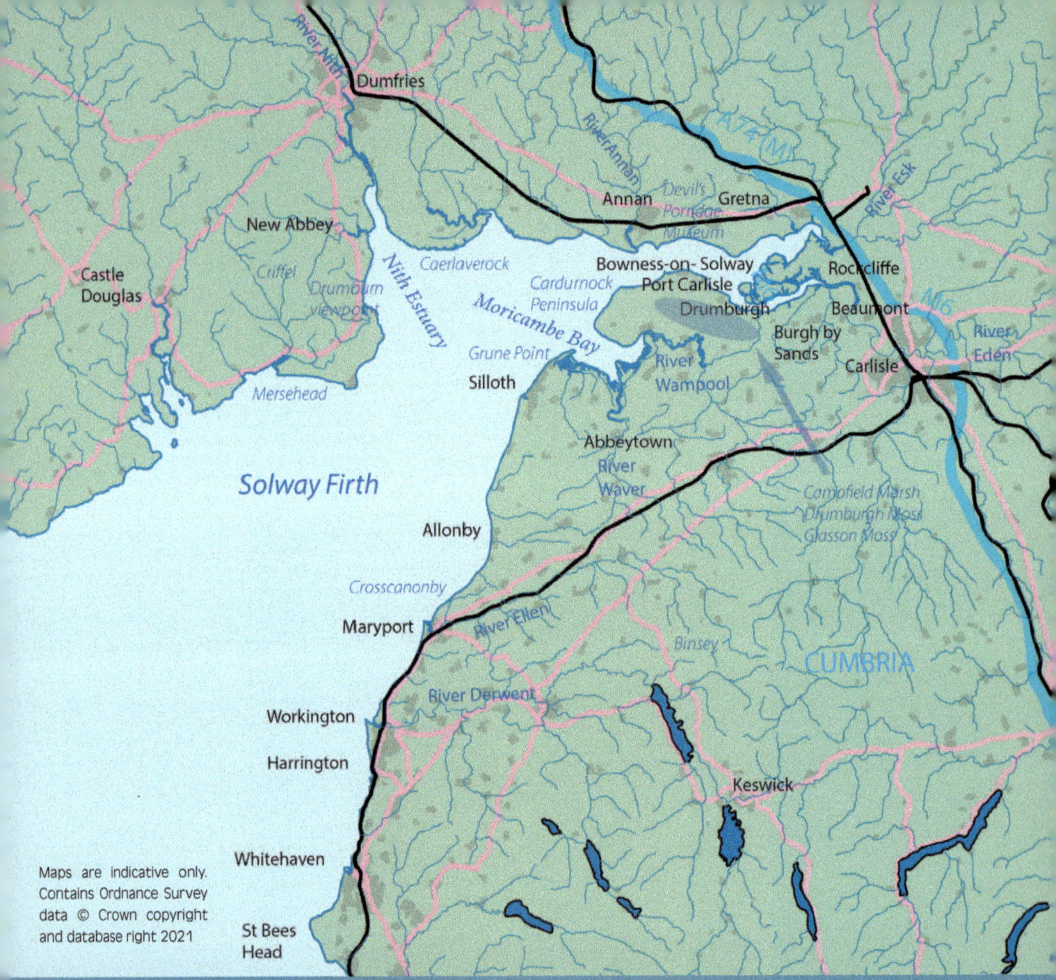

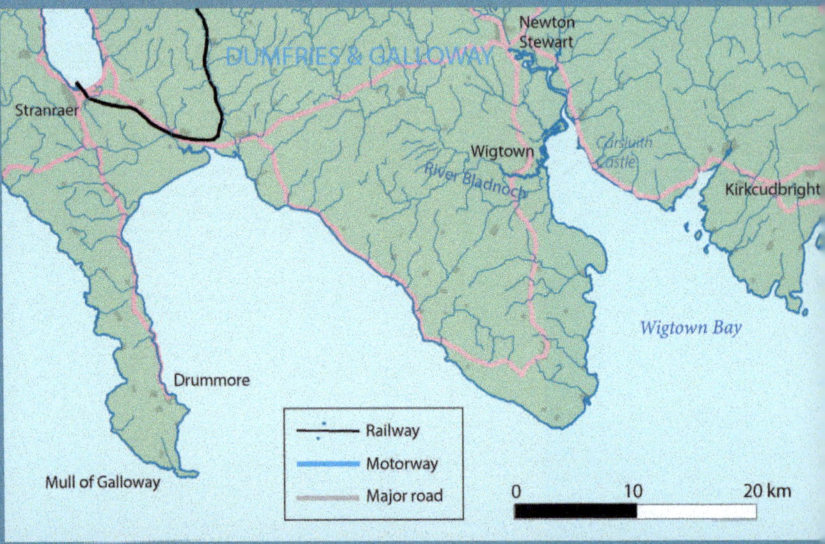

Solway Firth west of Castle Douglas ▶

▲ Panorama photo of the tidal Solway Firth © Dr Bruce G. Marcot (www.plexuseco.com/EPOW)

The Solway Firth extends from the spectacular sandstone cliffs of St Bees Head in Cumbria to Scotland's southernmost point, the Mull of Galloway, about fifty miles away. The Lake District fells and the hills of Dumfries and Galloway are an ever-present backdrop to the waterside views. On the highest tides, tidal bores make their way into several of the rivers around its shores. Wildlife highlights include the seabirds that nest on sea cliffs and occasional sightings of dolphins and porpoises.

The outer parts of the Solway Firth, south of Silloth and west of Dumfries, have a coastal feel, with cliffs, sand dunes and long expanses of beaches. The main ports in Cumbria grew on the wealth from coal mining, but commercial shipping is now confined to fishing fleets at Whitehaven, Maryport and Silloth and cargo vessels at Workington and Silloth. On the Scottish shores, harbours and ports include those at Annan and Kirkcudbright.

The upper part of the Solway Firth is more typical of an estuary, with large expanses of mudflats, sandbanks and saltmarsh exposed at low tide. This begins at Moricambe Bay, a shallow tidal inlet near Silloth, and extends to the Nith Estuary, near Dumfries. Sights in this part of the Solway include medieval churches, nature reserves and the historic towns of Annan and Dumfries.

Large numbers of migratory wading birds arrive in autumn and winter, including dunlins, knots, curlews and oystercatchers. Thousands of barnacle geese spend the winter here too, flying in from the Norwegian Arctic and forming spectacular formations at dawn and dusk.

Lowland raised mires are a feature of the Cumbrian shores and once stretched in an almost unbroken line along the coastal plain. These shelter many rare species of insects, plants and birds. Several nature reserves have been established to protect the areas that remain following industrial-scale peat extraction last century.

The tidal influence ends just to the west of Carlisle on the River Eden, Cumbria's largest river. Interesting places to visit in the city include its castle, cathedral and the Tullie House Museum & Art Gallery. Hadrian's Wall extended west through the city to Bowness-on-Solway with coastal defences continuing to Whitehaven and many signs remain of the Roman presence.

Criffel from Maryport Harbour

CUMBRIA SHORES

FEATURED LISTINGS

Bird's eye views	Binsey
Museums	The Beacon Museum, Whitehaven
	The Rum Story, Whitehaven
	Maryport Maritime Museum
	Solway Coast Discovery Centre, Silloth
	Tullie House Museum & Art Gallery
Maritime connections	St Bees Lighthouse
	Port Carlisle
Wildlife	St Bees Head
	Campfield Marsh
	Glasson Moss
Historic buildings	Holme Cultram Abbey
	St Michael's Church
Ancient sites	Roman fort, Maryport
	Milefortlet21
	Crosscanonby Saltpans
	King Edward I Monument, Burgh-by-Sands
Waterside walks and seaside resorts	Allonby
	Silloth
Tidal bore viewpoints	Wampool Estuary
	Drumburgh

THE CUMBRIA AND LAKE DISTRICT COAST

INTRODUCTION
The Cumbrian shores of the Solway Firth stretch from the dramatic cliffs of St Bees Head to the outskirts of Gretna in Scotland.

Major towns include the ports of Whitehaven, Workington and Maryport and the seaside resorts of Allonby and Silloth. Carlisle lies just upstream of the Solway Firth and Carlisle Canal once provided ships with a route to the city.

Other highlights include medieval churches, lowland raised mires and the remains of Roman coastal defences. In autumn and winter, large numbers of barnacle geese and other waterbirds visit the sands and mudflats of the upper estuary.

Solway Firth boundaries Along the Solway Firth there is a transition from the open coastline around St Bees Head and the Mull of Galloway to the inner or upper estuary east of Grune Point and the Nith Estuary. In scientific studies, zones are often defined to reflect these different characteristics.

Several definitions are used. In Scottish Government publications, the Solway Estuary is defined as extending from Cargo, west of Carlisle, to Dubmill Point, north of Allonby, and to Southerness, close to Dumfries. However, this term is not widely used outside scientific discussions.

The concept of an inner or upper estuary is more widespread, as used in this guide. For example, when planning the Solway Firth Marine Conservation Zone, the inner estuary was defined as extending from Grune Point to the tidal limit near Carlisle.

▼ Cliffs at St Bees Head (left) and guillemots roosting on the ledges (right)

SOLWAY FIRTH | 159

Places of interest

The outer Solway Firth

St Bees Head to Whitehaven

The Solway Firth begins at the spectacular sandstone cliffs of **St Bees Head**. These lie just north of the town of St Bees, which is described in Chapter 3, Irish Sea.

The cliffs are separated into two parts by Fleswick Bay. North of the bay, close to the highest point, St Bees Lighthouse still guides ships along these shores. The first lighthouse was coal-fired and began operation in 1718, and the current electric-powered light was automated in 1987. St Bees Head Foghorn Station, perching on the cliff edge nearby, is now disused, but once provided an audible warning in mist and fog. It is sometimes open to the public on Heritage Open Days (www.heritageopendays.org.uk).

▲ St Bees Head Foghorn Station

From the top of the cliffs there are great views along the coast and the Isle of Man is visible on a clear day. The RSPB has installed several viewing platforms giving vertiginous views of the seabirds that nest here. The cliff walk is steep in places and can be muddy at times, so suitable clothing and footwear is essential.

Whitehaven

Whitehaven marks the start of a more industrialised stretch of coastline, which extends as far as Maryport.

Here the sandstone rock that underlies much of west Cumbria gives way to carboniferous limestone. This contains coal deposits and Whitehaven became established on the wealth from coal mining, along with its neighbours to the north, Harrington, Workington and Maryport. Low-lying cliffs give interesting coastal views along much of this shoreline.

Whitehaven was a planned town initially designed in the 17th century by local landowner Sir John Lowther. It has several impressive Georgian buildings, with the broad streets of the town centre set out on a grid pattern. A fishing fleet operates from the attractive harbour. This includes a central pier with a covered viewing platform called the Crow's Nest.

The Beacon Museum lies alongside the historic harbour, with exciting displays and exhibitions telling the story of west Cumbria and the district of Copeland through local history and culture, from prehistory, Roman, Norse and beyond. The museum floors have been revitalised through a series of new interactive displays modernising the exhibitions and bringing them into the 21st century.

It also describes the history of the Sellafield site, which is a major employer in the region, and more recent developments in renewable energy. The purpose-built museum is housed in a cylindrical shaped building that looks like a lighthouse. A viewing platform

▲ (Top to bottom) The distinctive lighthouse shape of the Beacon Museum overlooking Whitehaven Harbour (© The Beacon Museum); View north along the coast from Whitehaven Harbour

at the top has panoramic views of the harbour. The ground floor includes a visitor information point for the west coast of Cumbria and there is a gift shop and harbourside restaurant too (www.thebeacon-whitehaven.co.uk).

A path above the museum leads to a great viewpoint on a headland, with a prominent tower called the Candlestick. This was once a ventilation chimney for the pit head of Wellington colliery,

▲ The Candlestick in Whitehaven

▲ (Top to bottom) Boats in the Derwent Estuary in Workington; View north from Harrington Harbour

whose deep-sea mine shafts began here, and in 1910 was the site of one of the UK's worst mining disasters. A white-painted building nearby was part of the pit works and unusually is decorated with a castellated roof, to make it look like a castle. The pit was closed in the 1930s and a mosaic next to the Candlestick commemorates the miners who worked here.

Within the town, **The Rum Story** exhibition describes the role of rum making and smuggling in the growth of the port. Set in the former warehouses of a local merchant, it is an imaginative record of that time, and includes the company's original office with authentic Georgian era fittings. Lifesize figures illustrate how rum is made and there are poignant reminders of the slave trade, including a replica of a tropical forest. Refreshments are available in the inner courtyard and there is a gift shop too (www.rumstory.co.uk; www.whitehavenhc.org.uk).

Workington and Harrington

To the north, **Workington** is the largest town around the Solway Firth and a major port. It lies at the mouth of the Derwent Estuary. The River Derwent is one of Cumbria's largest rivers whose source is near Keswick, in some of the

Lake District's finest scenery. It is joined by the River Cocker in Cockermouth, which flows down from two beautiful lakes, Buttermere and Crummock Water.

There has been a settlement here since Roman times, but as at Whitehaven the main growth was founded on coal mining. The manufacture of iron and steel then took over once the pits started to close.

The **Helena Thompson Museum** describes the industrial, social and cultural history of the town and includes an extensive collection of costumes, furniture and tableware. There is also a display about **Workington Hall**, a grand stately home dating back to the 14th century whose ruins lie nearby. The museum is housed in an elegant Georgian building gifted to the town in 1940 by local philanthropist Helena Thompson (www.helenathompson.org.uk).

The impressive remains of the hall lie in the grounds of Workington Hall Parklands (www.allerdale.gov.uk).

The docks block access to the northern shores of the Derwent Estuary, but there are footpaths and cycleways along the southern shores. A pier continues to a square shaped dock building with views of the town and coast. The letters 'C2C' painted on the side indicate that this is a starting point for the Coast to Coast cycleway, a spectacular route across the Lake District and Pennines finishing at Sunderland or Tynemouth (www.sustrans.org.uk).

On the outskirts of the town, **Siddick Ponds Local Nature Reserve** is a popular place to watch wildlife, with ponds, reed beds and grassland on a reclaimed industrial site. Many bird species have been spotted here, as well as otters, stoats and weasels (www.siddickponds.co.uk).

Harrington, which lies to the south of Workington, is now almost part of the town. It too once had a busy port founded on coal mining and steelmaking. Nowadays the harbour is a picturesque place to wander, particularly during the annual Kite Festival.

Maryport

The town of **Maryport** with its beautiful harbour and waterfront is just a few miles to the north. It lies at the mouth of the River Ellen, which is not usually considered as an estuary although the tidal influence extends a short way inland. The Ellen rises in hills in the northern Lake District.

Maryport, like Whitehaven, is a planned town, and was developed in the 18th century by landowner Humphrey Senhouse who named it after his wife Mary.

Many of the main attractions lie within or close to the harbour (www.visitallerdale.co.uk). The **Lake District Coast Aquarium** is a great place to find

▼ The waterfront at Maryport

▲ The tidal reaches of the River Ellen in Maryport; the sculpture is called 'A Fishy Tale' by Colin Telfor and is a tribute to the fishermen of the town

▲ (Above) Maryport Harbour from cliffs to the north; (Below) Senhouse Roman Museum

out more about the marine life of the Solway Firth and beyond. The shark and ray tank and regular talks and fish feeding sessions are particularly popular. Other highlights include Sea Lab, with displays including lobster breeding and jellyfish culture. There are also representative displays of native freshwater, tropical marine and tropical freshwater species. There is tourist information available, a café with harbour views, a gift shop, a fishing bait and tackle shop and a 14 hole crazy golf course (www.coastaquarium.co.uk).

Nearby, **Maryport Maritime Museum** describes the history of the port and the social and industrial history of the town (www.maryportmaritimemuseum.co.uk). Items on display include historic photographs and paintings of the port and models of ships built in the town. The town has a busy fishing fleet and the annual trawler race is a popular event.

High on a hill overlooking the harbour, the fabulous **Senhouse Roman Museum** describes the Roman occupation along these shores. The earthworks of a Roman fort lie in a field behind and artefacts on display include Roman altars and religious sculptures excavated from the fort and the civilian settlement to the north. The building was once a naval training centre and there are great views of the coast and harbour from a watchtower in the main compound (www.senhousemuseum.co.uk).

Maryport to Allonby

Heading north from Maryport, a wide promenade leads below low cliffs, giving a pleasant coastal walk. A line of sandy beaches then fringes the shoreline, backed by sand dunes in places.

Three miles north of the town lie the **Crosscanonby Salt Pans**, which were built in the 17th century. The main settling tank is a circular pan nearly eighteen metres across. Clay-lined cobble walls contained saltwater fed in from a smaller tank which was heated with charcoal. Salt was an important commodity used for preserving meat and fish. The site was used for about a century before succumbing to competition from rock salt mines in Cheshire. It was one of the last built around the Solway Firth in a tradition that stretches back several hundred years.

On a small hill overlooking the site is **Milefortlet 21**. This was one of the smaller forts in the Roman coastal defences. The earthworks have been uncovered to show a thick defensive wall surrounded by a moat or ditch. A main gate faced toward the coast, connected to a smaller gate at the rear by a central passageway. An artist's impression on one of the interpretation panels at the site suggests that the fort was a substantial structure, with turreted walls surrounding a barracks, commander's quarters and watchtower. See the Solway Coast AONB website for more details on both sites (www.solwaycoastaonb.org.uk).

A short way north is the coastal resort of **Allonby** (www.allonbycumbria.co.uk). Established in Georgian and Victorian times, its brightly painted houses are typical of the area. Nowadays the beach is popular with holidaymakers and wind- and kite-surfers. The village lies on a wide sweeping bay that viewed from its northern end has a dramatic backdrop

(Above) Crosscanonby Saltpans; (Below) Milefortlet 21 ▶

▲ Silloth promenade

of Lake District fells. A small river called Allonby Beck reaches the coast here.

Silloth

To the north, **Silloth** became established as a seaside resort in Victorian times. The small harbour is home to a fishing fleet and leads to an enclosed dock for cargo vessels.

Highlights of the town include the promenade and the elegant cobbled main street. **Silloth Green** alongside is a large grassy area with a glass-fronted pavilion on a low hill overlooking the promenade.

Telephoto view of Allonby against distant Lakeland fells ▼

This is the Victorian Pagoda and has great views across the Solway Firth to the hills of Dumfries and Galloway. Information panels inside have images showing the local history of the town. The town is laid out on a grid pattern and the streets leading off the main street are named after rivers that drain into the Solway Firth and the River Eden.

There is a good choice of cafés and the traditional trappings of a seaside resort, such as ice cream parlours and a fairground. Some attractions are seasonal so check opening times before travelling. A busy events schedule includes the Silloth Carnival and a community

▼ The Victorian Pagoda at Silloth

▲ Telephoto view at low tide across the Solway Firth from Allonby

despite its similar name has no connection with Morecambe Bay. The rivers Waver and Wampool flow into the bay and at low tide their channels snake across the mudflats. Both rivers rise in low hills north of the Lake District. A row of posts in the bay was installed for target practice in World War 2 and are now often frequented by cormorants.

Footpaths and minor roads around the bay are susceptible to flooding, and warning signs, embankments and

festival called Silloth Green Day (www.visitallerdale.co.uk).

The **Solway Coast Discovery Centre** is home to the Silloth Library, tourist information centre and an exhibition highlighting the wildlife, heritage and landscape of the Solway Firth. It also includes some local history models on the history of Silloth, including the railway that once stopped here and the former military airfield on the outskirts of the town. Find out more by searching on 'Discovery Centre' at www.solwaycoastaonb.org.uk.

The upper Solway Firth
Moricambe Bay/Cardurnock Peninsula

The promenade in Silloth heads north toward the settlement of Skinburness. Footpaths then lead to **Grune Point**, a stony peninsula with areas of grassland, scrub and fields, flanked by shingle beaches. It is a good place for watching wading birds in winter.

Grune Point forms the western boundary of Moricambe Bay, which

▲ (Top to bottom) Shingle beach at Grune Point; the building is a military installation (pill box) from World War 2; View across Moricambe Bay from the Cardurnock Peninsula

floodgates reinforce the danger. The main road out of Silloth heads further inland to Abbeytown, the site of 12th century **Holme Cultram Abbey**. Once one of the most powerful religious foundations in Cumbria, the abbey's wealth was founded on sheep and cattle rearing and the wool trade. The abbey's impact on the landscape included draining marshes and cutting down woods to make land for agriculture and grazing. Following the dissolution of the monasteries in the 16th century, the nave was preserved and is now used as a church (www.solwaycoastaonb.org.uk).

The opposite shores of Moricambe Bay are enclosed by the **Cardurnock Peninsula**. Anthorn is the only significant village and several radio towers nearby are visible for miles around. These are situated on a former military airfield and one of the masts transmits the time signal for the whole of the UK. This is widely used by government and businesses and gives the time reference for radio-controlled clocks and watches. A scenic coastal road heads around the peninsula, with dramatic views across the Solway Firth to the hills of Dumfries and Galloway throughout the year, and in the summer glorious displays of gorse.

Cardurnock Peninsula to Beaumont

The Solway Firth has much more of an estuarine feel beyond the Cardurnock Peninsula, with the opposite shores now closer and large areas of sandbanks and mudflats exposed at low tide. Extensive areas of saltmarsh fringe the shores.

Inland, lowland raised mires are a major feature, such as at the RSPB's **Campfield Marsh Nature Reserve**. This

▲ (Top to bottom) Radio towers at Anthorn viewed across the River Wampool; Holme Cultram Abbey; the sign reads 'Welcome to Holme Cultram 12th century Cicstercian Abbey Parish Church of St Mary the Virgin'; St John's Church at Newton Arlosh

▲ Start of the Hadrian's Wall Path at Bowness-on-Solway

is an area of saltmarsh, wetlands and ponds, with a mire under restoration. The main walkway leads up to a low hill, which is a good viewpoint for this part of the estuary and the hills of Dumfries and Galloway. More information on the reserve is given later.

Not far beyond, the village of **Bowness-on-Solway** lies on the estuary shores. This was the westernmost point on Hadrian's Wall and there was once a large Roman fort here. The fort was built to defend a low tide fording point from Annan across the Solway Firth. Known locally as a *wath*, from the Old Norse word for ford, this crossing and others to the east remain highly dangerous and there have been many tragedies over the years.

Few signs remain of the Roman presence but the village is now the starting point for the Hadrian's Wall Path that follows the route of the wall to the North Sea coast. An elegant wooden shelter marks the start, with information boards that describe the route and the local wildlife. This lies on The Banks, a community garden and promenade which provides great views of the estuary and hills beyond. An inscription on the shelter includes the following good luck message in Latin, with an English translation: *Wallsend 84 miles. Good luck go with you. Segedvno Mp LXXXIIII Fortvna vobis adsit.*

The next village along the coast is **Port Carlisle**. There are still signs of the port that was once here, although the canal that provided a connection to Carlisle was built over by a railway, itself now dismantled. The ruins of the harbour

These pillars near Bowness-on-Solway once supported a viaduct for the Solway Junction Railway over the Solway Firth to Annan, which was built to transport iron ore to Scotland. It was demolished in the 1930s ▼

walls are now a haven for waterbirds, such as redshanks and oystercatchers.

Soon after Port Carlisle, the coastal road passes through the small village of **Drumburgh**. Here a raised area provides good views of the estuary, with an information board that describes the local history and wildlife. It is a great place to see the Solway Tidal Bore, which is described later. An impressive 14th century stone building called Drumburgh Castle is in fact a fortified farmhouse. It was built near the ruins of a small Roman fort here that guarded another low tide route across the Solway.

Fortified buildings are a common sight in north Cumbria and another impressive example is the 12th century **St Michael's Church** in nearby Burgh by Sands. In medieval times it provided a place of refuge during border raids, with a fortified tower where villagers could shelter. The church was built on the site of another Roman fort, which again was linked to defending a low tide crossing. Stones from the fort were used in its construction.

King Edward I died of illness on the saltmarshes near here in 1307 while travelling north with his army and his body lay in state in the church before final burial in Westminster Abbey. The **King Edward I Monument** on the marsh was built in the 17th century near where he fell and is a popular spot to visit. However, great care must be taken not to be caught out by the tides, checking tide times before setting off.

Heading toward Carlisle, Beaumont is the last large village on the southern shores of the Solway Firth. It lies on a hill overlooking the River Eden. Medieval St

▲ (Top to bottom) Warning signs highlight that the road immediately east from Drumburgh is prone to tidal flooding; Drumburgh Castle in the setting sun; The King Edward I Monument

Mary's Church is near the centre of the village.

Rockcliffe to the Scottish Border

On the highest tides, the tidal influence in the Solway extends as far inland as the village of Cargo, which lies slightly upstream of Beaumont on the opposite shores, about three miles west of Carlisle. The name Cargo is derived from the Celtic word for rock and the Old Norse for hill.

A minor road leads to the village of **Rockcliffe**. Like Beaumont, this is situated above the floodplain, with an impressive church. The village is close to Rockcliffe Marsh, which is the largest area of saltmarsh around the Solway Firth.

The marsh is often flooded at high tide and extensive earth embankments help to reduce the flood risk inland. Most of the marsh is private land used for grazing, although guided tours are occasionally organised by Cumbria Wildlife Trust, who maintain a warden there in spring and summer to monitor and protect the many nesting birds. In winter, large numbers of wading birds roost on the marshes at high tide. The Castletown Estate owns much of the marsh and surrounding farmland.

To the north, the marsh is bounded by the River Esk, which flows down from Scotland. The Scottish border is a short way beyond, just before the town of Gretna, and marks the end of the Cumbrian shores of the Solway Firth.

The City of Carlisle

As the only city in Cumbria, **Carlisle** is a major regional centre. It lies just inland from the start of the Solway Firth but

▲ (Above) St Michael's Church at Burgh by Sands; (Below) Cattle on Rockcliffe Marsh

once played a key role in maritime trade via a canal link to Port Carlisle.

Popular tourist destinations include the Guildhall Museum, **Carlisle Cathedral**, Carlisle Castle, and the Tullie House Museum & Art Gallery. Waterside walks are popular and the River Eden is particularly scenic as it passes through the city. The tourist information centre is situated in the Old Town Hall, itself an interesting building dating from the 17th century.

Nearby, the **Guildhall Museum** is situated on the upper floors of an elegant 15th century restored timber-framed building. This is one of the oldest remaining in the city and retains some of the original wattle and daub (mud on timber) wall structure. The museum describes the history of the city's guilds who regulated and protected trades such as shoemaking, tanning and weaving. The upper floors are overhanging, which was common in medieval times when buildings were taxed on the area of the ground floor.

The 12th century cathedral has a spectacular arched ceiling decorated with angels and stars. Below ground, the Treasury exhibition has many historic items on display from the cathedral and local parishes. Impressive stained-glass windows and intricate artwork are other features. A covered courtyard café adjoins the historic Fratry building, which in medieval times was the dining hall for the Cathedral Priory (www.carlislecathedral.org.uk).

Carlisle Castle is just outside the city centre with dungeons, narrow passageways and stone chambers to explore (www.english-heritage.org.uk). In the grounds, Cumbria's Museum of Military Life describes the history of the county's infantry regiment over the past three hundred years (www.cumbriasmuseumofmilitarylife.org).

The excellent **Tullie House Museum & Art Gallery** lies within sight of the castle, with exhibits on local history, culture, wildlife and geology. An entire floor is dedicated to Roman history, including items on loan from the British

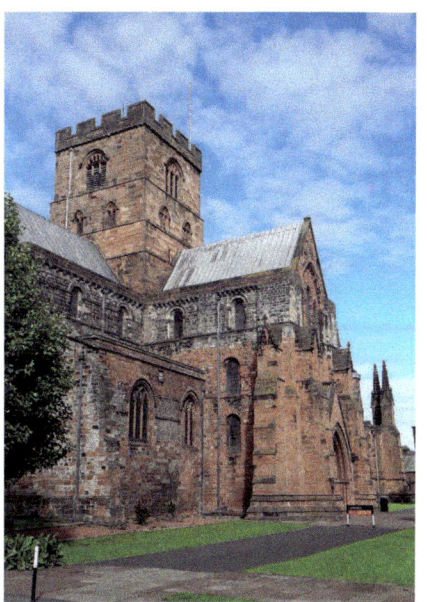

▲ (Above) Carlisle Cathedral; (Below) Street view in Carlisle

Museum. Other galleries show fine art and decorative art, plus costumes and textiles from the region.

On the top floor, an elevated viewpoint looks out over the castle, while in the street outside decorated paving stones show the key forts along Hadrian's Wall. The café specializes in local products and includes a terrace in the museum garden. Also in the grounds, the 17th century Old Tullie House is part of the museum and hosts a regular programme of talks and events (www.tulliehouse.co.uk).

Carlisle Castle ▼

▲ The Guildhall Museum in Carlisle

COASTAL VIEWPOINTS

The northern fells of the Lake District rise from the coastal plain of the Solway Firth, giving views of its shores and of the hills of Dumfries and Galloway beyond.

If travelling by road, there are distant views from some of the minor roads through hills to the north of Caldbeck, in the Lake District. However, perhaps the best viewpoint is Binsey (447m), a low-lying isolated fell on the outer edges of the national park. This is the one of the most northerly of the 214 Wainwrights, named after hillwalker Alfred Wainwright, who wrote a landmark series of walking guides to the Lake District.

▲ Telephoto view of the Solway Firth from low hills in north Cumbria

One popular route starts from near Binsey Lodge and follows grassy slopes to the top. The terrain can be slippery and boggy in places so a map and appropriate hillwalking clothing and footwear are required. From the summit there are fabulous views inland toward Bassenthwaite and the Lake District, and north to the Solway Firth and beyond.

For a different type of experience, it is worth visiting the sea cliffs at St Bees Head, which provide superb views along the coast as described earlier.

▼ The Solway Firth and Criffel from Binsey

SOURCE TO SEA: RIVER EDEN

Many rivers flow into the Solway Firth and the largest is the River Eden, which is also Cumbria's largest river. The beautiful Eden Valley is a great place to visit for its many historical sites and hillwalking and cycling opportunities (www.visiteden.co.uk).

The Eden rises in the Yorkshire Dales on the marshes and bogs of Mallerstang Common. It then flows through Mallerstang Valley between the imposing cliffs of Mallerstang Edge and the long ridge of Wild Boar Fell.

The countryside then becomes more open, with the north Pennine hills ever present to the east, whose high point is Cross Fell (893m). Major settlements include Kirkby Stephen, Appleby-in-Westmorland and Carlisle. The picturesque Settle to Carlisle Railway follows the river for much of its course as do the Eden Benchmarks, an imaginative series of ten sculptures that start high in the Mallerstang Valley and end at Rockcliffe alongside the Solway Firth.

Historic sites include Pendragon Castle, near Kirkby Stephen, Appleby Castle, and Carlisle's castle and cathedral. Several major tributaries join the Eden along its course, such as the rivers Eamont and Lowther, which flow down from two of the Lake District's largest and most beautiful lakes, Ullswater and Haweswater. The tributary valleys have their own attractions including castles, waterfalls, nature reserves, and watermills. The market town of Penrith is a popular base for exploring the area.

The tidal influence begins near Cargo to the west of Carlisle, and the Eden takes on a more estuarine feel alongside Cumbria's largest saltmarsh, Rockcliffe Marsh. The River Esk flows into the Solway Firth from the other side of the marsh and rises in Scotland's mountains.

Other rivers that flow into the Solway Firth further west include the Waver and Wampool at Moricambe Bay and the Ellen and Derwent at Maryport and Workington. On the Scottish shores, major rivers include the Annan, Nith and Cree at Annan, Dumfries and Newton Stewart.

▲ (Top to bottom) The River Eden passes over Hell Gill Force waterfall before starting its journey to the coast; Watercut, an Eden Benchmark sculpture by Mary Bourne in Mallerstang Valley; Southeastern shores of Ullswater

The upper Eden viewed from Mallerstang Edge; (Inset) Middle reaches of the River Eden

Maritime history

The Solway Firth has long been used for coastal trade. Perhaps the first harbour was that built by the Romans at Maryport. This supplied the fort and civilian town there and coastal defences to the north. Hadrian's Wall helped to guard against another threat, that of invasions over the sands at low tide at crossing points at Bowness-on-Solway, Drumburgh and near Burgh by Sands.

During medieval times, Holme Cultram Abbey traded wool, grain and salt from a port at Skinburness, which was relocated to Newton Arlosh in the 14th century due to storm damage. Recent excavations have discovered a wharf close to the abbey, suggesting that goods were transported to the coast along an old channel of the River Waver, which passes nearby (www.westcumbriaarchaeology.org).

Following the dissolution of the monasteries in the 16th century, Old Sandsfield near Burgh by Sands became established as a port for Carlisle merchants, including shipments from Liverpool. Rockcliffe on the opposite shores was briefly a port too.

A disadvantage was that goods had to be transported by land between the port and the city. Another problem was that the shifting sands and strong currents placed limits on the size of vessels, so a canal was built to Port Carlisle for access to deeper water. Initially trade was brisk and included passenger services to Annan, Whitehaven and Liverpool. However, by the mid-19th century the canal was closed due to competition from the railways.

▲ Tall ships in Whitehaven Harbour; a reminder of bygone days

Instead, the fishing port at Silloth was developed as a port for Carlisle, and once had a railway connection. Some goods are still imported via the port, although its main role is to serve a factory alongside the dock. There is a small fishing fleet that specializes in shrimp. One reminder of the early days is the two lights that help with navigation at night, in addition to modern electronic aids. These are the Lees Scar Lighthouse, southwest of the port entrance, and East Cote Lighthouse, on land next to the promenade. Both are mounted on metal frames.

Further south, coal mining began on an industrial scale in the 18th century. The coal deposits extended from Maryport to Whitehaven. Ports were established there and at Harrington and Workington in between and the story of this remarkable transformation is described in the following section.

Several museums around the Solway Firth have interesting exhibits on local maritime history, including Maryport Maritime Museum, the Beacon Museum in Whitehaven, Tullie House Museum & Art Gallery in Carlisle, Annan Museum and Dumfries Museum. Chapter 1, Coastal themes, discusses this topic further as well as the challenges involved in navigating the Cumbrian coastline.

▲ Coastal shipping viewed from Whitehaven Harbour

Shipping and mining

In west Cumbria, large-scale coal mining began in the 17th century and ports were developed along the line of coal deposits, which extend roughly from Whitehaven to Maryport.

The scale of activity is difficult to imagine nowadays, but included coal and limestone exports, with particularly close links with Ireland. As trade grew, more piers and quays were added and enclosed docks with gates were built, allowing ships to unload unaffected by the tides. Paintings from the early years suggest that the forest of masts of sailing ships in port must have made an impressive sight.

Over time, dredging and enclosed docks allowed larger vessels to be accommodated, which from the early 19th century included steamships. By the end of the century, blast-furnace and pit-ventilation chimneys dotted the skyline and railway tracks extended up to the ports. The ready availability of steel and coal spurred the growth of shipbuilding and other manufactured goods that were traded worldwide.

The pattern of development varied between ports. In **Whitehaven**, the first quay was built early in the 17th century to export salt and coal. By the middle of the 18th century Whitehaven was the third busiest port in England after London and Bristol, in part through the slave trade, handling tobacco, rum and sugar. In the 19th century, steamships operated to several destinations around the Irish Sea,

The mouth of the Derwent Estuary and entrance to the Port of Workington, with a windfarm in the distance ▼

including Liverpool, Dublin, Dumfries and the Isle of Man.

However, trade began to decrease with the advent of the railways and the decline of coal mining, although coastal shipping continued on a small scale until the 1990s. The last coal mine was closed in the 1980s. Nowadays, the town has a picturesque harbour and marina, overlooked by the Beacon Museum. A pair of lighthouses guard the harbour entrance, one in the classical shape of a tapered column with a light and domed roof, and the other a more solid cylindrical structure with a flat top.

Heading north, the first pier in **Harrington** was built in the mid-18th century to handle coal; steelmaking and a shipbuilding industry followed. Photographs taken at its peak show the harbour surrounded by industrial works, railway lines and factory chimneys.

By the early 1900s trade was

▲ St Bees Lighthouse

Maryport Harbour ▼

beginning to decline. In World War 2 the harbour was sealed off to use as a reservoir for a nearby factory which was extracting magnesium from seawater for use in aircraft components and incendiary bombs. Nowadays, most of the industrial sites have been cleared and the harbour is a picturesque spot to visit.

The largest port nowadays is **Workington**, just to the north of Harrington. From the 17th century it traded mainly in coal but as coal mining declined from the mid-19th century, iron and steelmaking and shipbuilding took over. These continued as major industries

▲ Whitehaven Harbour

CARLISLE CANAL

Carlisle Canal was opened in 1823 to provide a link from Carlisle to Fisher's Cross on the shores of the Solway Firth. The village was renamed as Port Carlisle after the canal was built. Ocean-going vessels could now reach Carlisle and facilities included a dock basin, warehouses and a shipbuilding yard. The site of the basin was behind a modern-day landmark, the McVitie's biscuit factory near the city centre.

The canal was just over eleven miles long and more than fifty feet wide. It descended by sixty feet along its course and had eight locks, two in Port Carlisle and six about halfway along. Water was supplied from a small reservoir and pumped flows from the River Eden.

Early trade included the transport of coal and then bricks, with passenger services to Annan, Dumfries, Whitehaven and Liverpool. Steamships would berth at a pier near the canal entrance to board passengers arriving by packet boat from Carlisle. However, competition from the railways began to affect trade and by 1846 the canal company was looking into a range of options, including the radical idea of selling the canal so that a railway could be built along its path.

▲ The former entrance to the Carlisle Canal

That was the option chosen and in 1854 the Port Carlisle branch line opened providing rail connections to both Carlisle and Silloth. Few signs remain of the canal nowadays, although remnants of the stone outer dock, canal entrance and steamship pier uprights are still visible at Port Carlisle. The railway is long gone too.

SOLWAY TIDAL BORE

On the highest tides, a well-developed wave forms on the Solway, starting a short way downstream from Bowness-on-Solway. Here it is well offshore in the main channel and may only be visible with binoculars or a telescope. In light winds, it can sometimes be heard in the distance. One viewpoint is the small car park at the western end of the village, used as a turning point by local buses.

Passing Port Carlisle, the bore is still distant but at Drumburgh comes closer to the shore, by now sometimes a well-defined line of surf. Perhaps the best viewing point is a small grass-covered area to the east of the village, on a slight rise above the saltmarshes, from where the wave can be seen approaching and then disappearing off into the distance. Be aware that the road east from here toward Carlisle is low lying and liable to flood on high tides, as evidenced by the warning signs to drivers. At its most powerful, the Solway Bore makes it past Old Sandsfield to the village of Rockcliffe, opposite Beaumont.

This is the main tidal bore on the Solway Firth, but others form on several of its tributaries. In Cumbria, a smaller wave forms on the Wampool, visible near the road bridge over the river on the main coastal road, at the top of Moricambe Bay. Tidal bores also form in some Scottish rivers around the Solway Firth as discussed later.

As with many natural phenomena, it requires some luck to spot a tidal bore, and there may only be a few days a year when conditions are right. Chapter 1, Coastal themes, discusses how tidal bores form and gives tips on viewpoints and where to find out tide times. It also discusses water safety when watching tidal bores, in particular the need to watch from a site above high water level and never venture out onto the sands, mudflats or saltmarsh.

The Solway Bore at Port Carlisle (left), Rockcliffe (right) and Drumburgh (lower) ▼

until the 1980s. Today the port remains busy with coastal trade and support vessels for offshore windfarms in the Solway Firth, with rail connections to the main railway network.

Leisure craft moor in a side channel of the Derwent and yachts berth in a marina opposite the port near the estuary mouth.

Maryport is the most northerly of the four main ports along this stretch of coastline. The port was established in the 18th century, with coal and shipbuilding the main activities, and iron and steelmaking in later years. Shipbuilding continued up to the early 1900s and commercial traffic until the 1960s. The last deep pit mine closed in that decade. A fishing fleet still operates here and there is a busy marina.

Wildlife

The Solway Firth is famed for its wading birds and wildfowl. At low tide large areas of mudflats and sandbanks are exposed, along with saltmarsh. These provide rich feeding grounds for migratory birds.

The most famous visitors are the barnacle geese that spend the winter here before returning to the Arctic again in spring. Numbers exceed forty thousand

▲ A Solway Coast AONB sign with the Solway Firth and Criffel in the background

in some years, forming spectacular formations as they fly to and from their feeding grounds at dawn and dusk. The cliffs of St Bees Head are a great place for birdwatching, attracting huge numbers of guillemots, kittiwakes and other seabirds to nest in spring and summer.

The lowland raised mires, or mosses, on the southern shores are another important habitat. Although large areas have been lost to peat extraction, those that remain are rich in bird, plant and insect life, such as dragonflies, butterflies and the insect-eating sundew plant.

Sand dunes are another threatened habitat, with a similarly diverse range of plant and bird life. The best examples around the Solway Firth are at Grune

▼ Lapwings near Port Carlisle

Point near Silloth and Mawbray Banks near Allonby.

Chapter 1, Coastal themes, gives more background on the wildlife of the Solway Firth and Cumbria, including on lowland raised mires, saltmarsh and sand dunes.

It also discusses the types of marine life seen around the shoreline, such as dolphins, porpoises, seals and whales. Sightings from land are rare in the Solway Firth, but occasionally include dolphins and porpoises from St Bees Head and the cliffs north of Maryport, and porpoises from the promenade in Silloth.

Traditional haaf net fishing for salmon and sea trout, which may date from Viking times, is still practised in a few places in the upper Solway Firth, from the Cumbrian and Scottish shores. The nets are supported on frames and held upright to catch fish on the ebb and flood tides.

Nature reserves

The RSPB reserves at St Bees Head and Campfield Marsh are two of the best known along the southern coast of the Solway Firth.

The St Bees reserve is famed for its nesting seabirds while Campfield Marsh features a variety of coastal habitats, including part of the lowland raised mires that once stretched along these shores. Other remnants include those at **Drumburgh Moss** and **Glasson Moss**, which both feature walkways and viewing platforms to view the restored areas of peatland. The less-developed but larger Wedholme Flow site lies to the south. This is part of the South Solway

▲ Observation tower (upper) and walkway (lower) at Glasson Moss National Nature Reserve

▼ A flock of teal on Bowness Common

Mosses National Nature Reserve and the RSPB, Cumbria Wildlife Trust (www.cumbriawildlifetrust.org.uk) and Natural England websites have more details (www.gov.uk).

Other sites include **Bowness-on-Solway** (at a former quarry) and **Finglandrigg Wood**, west of Carlisle. Further west, other popular wildlife-watching sites include Grune Point and Moricambe Bay near Silloth and Siddick Ponds near Workington. On a larger scale, much of the northern coastline in Cumbria forms part of the Solway Coast AONB.

Solway Coast AONB

In recognition of its unique landscape and habitat, part of the Cumbrian shoreline of the Solway Firth is designated as an Area of Outstanding Natural Beauty. Together with national parks, AONBs represent the most outstanding landscapes in the UK, to be managed in the interest of everyone and protected for future generations. Highlights include historic sites dating back to Roman and medieval times and the huge variety of bird, insect and plant life in the diverse range of habitats found in this landscape.

The Solway Coast AONB was established in 1964 and extends from Maryport to Rockcliffe, taking in the coastal plain and inland around the main areas of lowland raised mires. Other rare habitat includes saltmarsh and sand dunes.

The area covered is about 115 km^2 and the AONB staff team operates from offices in Silloth. Activities include planning, project development, nature recovery and site management, supporting the growth of sustainable tourism, and coordinating volunteer activities. The office is next door to the excellent Solway Coast Discovery Centre described earlier.

The AONB publishes a series of guides to the area on topics such as birdwatching, wildflowers and walking and cycling routes, and most of these are available for download at www.solwaycoastaonb.org.uk.

RSPB Campfield Marsh Nature Reserve

The Campfield Marsh reserve is west of Bowness-on-Solway on the shores of the Solway Firth (www.rspb.org.uk). It has a visitor centre with information about the reserve and an exhibition on the wildlife of the Solway Firth. The reserve spans a range of habitats, from saltmarsh at the estuary shores to a mix of wet grassland, woodland, farmland and lowland raised mires. This results in a wide variety of plant, insect and bird life.

From the visitor centre, the longest trail leads past ponds and bird hides to woods, and then gently climbs along a raised wooden walkway across the peat

Oystercatchers and dunlins passing the RSPB Campfield Marsh reserve ▼

bog. From the end it is just a short walk to the hill top, with views toward the Solway Firth and the hills of Dumfries and Galloway. The hill is one of several drumlins left in the region following the last Ice Age, formed from a mound of rubble left by a retreating glacier.

In the summer, birds such as lapwings and curlews nest in the reserve, and in the winter large numbers of barnacle and pink-footed geese gather here. The ponds, wetland and peatbog attract a wide variety of dragonflies and butterflies in summer.

Just outside the entrance, saltmarsh stretches alongside the main road in both directions and forms part of the reserve. At high tide this is a great place for watching wading birds such as oystercatchers, curlews, grey plovers and dunlins as they are pushed toward the shoreline. Large numbers often gather here and at ponds in the marsh, or are seen flying along the coast.

RSPB St Bees Head Nature Reserve

The sandstone cliffs at St Bees Head are the highest cliffs in northwest England. During late spring and early summer, several thousand seabirds nest on their ledges, making a spectacular sight. Species include guillemots, kittiwakes, razorbills, fulmars and cormorants, while gannets and other seabirds are often spotted flying out at sea. About three pairs of black guillemots nest here too and are the only breeding pairs in England.

The cliffs can be reached by paths from the seafront at St Bees, and the RSPB has placed viewing platforms at key points to provide a good, if vertiginous, view of the nesting birds. The climb is steep in places, with steep drops nearby, and crosses a gully leading to Fleswick Bay along a potentially slippery path. Appropriate footwear is therefore required, with wet weather clothing if rain or snow threatens.

The high point beyond St Bees Lighthouse makes a pleasant detour after the nesting areas, with good views north along the coast past Whitehaven. The RSPB website gives details of the route, viewing platforms and walking safety (www.rspb.org.uk).

Guillemots at St Bees Head

Mull of Galloway Lighthouse

SCOTTISH SHORES

FEATURED LISTINGS

Bird's eye views	Criffel
Museums	Dumfries Museum
Maritime connections	Mull of Galloway
Wildlife	Caerlaverock
	Mersehead
	Mull of Galloway
Historic buildings	Sweetheart Abbey
Tidal bore viewpoints	Near Annan
	Glencaple, Nith Estuary
	Near Wigtown, Bladnoch Estuary

THE CUMBRIA AND LAKE DISTRICT COAST

> **INTRODUCTION**
> The Scottish shores of the Solway Firth extend from the outskirts of Gretna to the cliffs of the Mull of Galloway.
>   The coast lies entirely in Dumfries and Galloway and is an area of historic sites, coastal hills and remote beaches. Popular destinations include Gretna Green, Annan, Dumfries, Kirkcudbright and Wigtown. The saltmarshes and mudflats of its estuaries provide rich feeding ground for waterbirds with several nature reserves.
>   The website of the Solway Firth Partnership (www.solwayfirthpartnership.co.uk) has an excellent guide to beaches in the area while the Visit Scotland and D&G online websites give more details on the many attractions at the coast and inland.

▲ Welcome sign in Gretna

Gretna to Annan

The town of Gretna is just over the border. The nearby village of **Gretna Green** became famous in the 18th century as a place for couples to elope to take advantage of Scotland's more lenient marriage laws. The **'Famous Blacksmiths Shop'** is a popular wedding venue and visitor attraction with gift shops, places to eat and a museum on the history of Gretna Green (www.gretnagreen.com).

Gretna itself is on the opposite side of the A75 and was built as a planned town in World War I to house workers at HM Factory Gretna, an extraordinary military complex extending nine miles to the west. The main product was cordite, which was used in ammunition and made by combining nitroglycerine and gun cotton, a highly dangerous process. After visiting as a War Correspondent, Sir Arthur Conan Doyle coined the name 'the devil's porridge' for this mixture and a fascinating modern museum of that name describes the history of the site. Other exhibits explore local contributions to the Cold War and both world wars, and a virtual reality tour of the inside of the decommissioned Chapelcross Nuclear Power Station outside Annan. It has a café and a gift shop too (www.devilsporridge.org.uk).

The **Devil's Porridge Museum** is situated in Eastriggs, which like Gretna was built to accommodate workers at the plant. It is close to the historic town of **Annan**, which has sandstone buildings dating back to the 18th century. The town was once an important port and a few craft still use the harbour, which lies on the estuary of the River Annan. **Annan Museum** describes the history of the town and port (www.dgculture.co.uk). The Annandale Distillery lies just outside the town, with pre-booked tours available (www.annandaledistillery.com).

▲ Distant Lake District fells viewed across the Esk near Annan; the birds are oystercatchers

RIDING OF THE MARCHES
Annan's annual Riding of the Marches event sees more than a hundred riders inspect the town boundaries on horseback. This is the centrepiece of a week of music and entertainment and part of a tradition that dates back more than 600 years. One highlight is a race across the sands of the Solway Firth at low tide.

Dumfries and the Nith Estuary

To the west is **Dumfries**, an attractive market town on the banks of the River Nith and the largest town in Dumfries and Galloway. At **Dumfries Museum**, an unusual domed tower alongside the main hall provides great views of the town. This was originally a windmill before it was converted to an observatory in the 1830s. It houses the Camera Obscura which uses an early astronomical technique to display a panoramic view of the area onto a concave, circular white table.

The museum explores local history and culture from prehistoric times, including exhibits on the wildlife of the Solway and life on a Victorian farm. Nearby, the **Old Bridge House Museum** describes everyday life in the past and is housed in one of the oldest buildings in the town (www.dgculture.co.uk).

On the banks of the Nith, the **Robert Burns Centre** celebrates the life of Scotland's national poet, who spent his final years at nearby **Robert Burns House**, which is also open to the public. Following a parade through the town centre, the annual Nithraid River Festival is held on the waterside Mill Green next to the centre. This includes a sailing and rowing boat race up the estuary from the coast (www.thestove.org).

The estuary is one of the largest around the Solway Firth and sights around its shores include **Caerlaverock Wetland Centre** (see later) and **Caerlaverock National Nature Reserve** (www.nature.scot). Historic Scotland sites include the impressive 13th century **Caerlaverock Castle** and **Sweetheart Abbey** and the

▲ (Top to bottom) Weir on the River Nith in Dumfries; The tower housing the Camera Obscura at Dumfries Museum; Caerlaverock Castle

restored 18th century **New Abbey Corn Mill** (www.historicscotland.gov.uk). The castle has a gatehouse, moat and curtain walls laid out on a triangular pattern and is on the eastern shores of the estuary. The abbey and the corn mill are in the village of New Abbey to the west.

Drumburn Viewpoint is a great place nearby for views of the Solway Firth, including the picturesque coastal village of Carsethorn. The RSPB **Mersehead Reserve** lies at the coast a short way beyond the estuary. Habitat includes wetlands, woods, farmland and extensive sandbanks which are exposed at low tide. Wildlife highlights include barnacle geese, natterjack toads, and many species of wading and woodland birds. Facilities include a visitor centre and two enclosed hides (www.rspb.org.uk). The term 'merse' is the local name for saltmarsh.

For views of the Solway Firth, **Criffel** (569m) near Dumfries is a superb vantage point. This hill is visible from much of the Cumbrian coastline, and its broad summit and slopes give it an imposing stature that draws the eye. The usual ascents are from New Abbey or a small parking area to the south of Loch Kindar. After passing through woods, the ascent becomes steep and is often boggy, requiring appropriate clothing, footwear and equipment. The climb is worth it though as the views from the top take in the Nith Estuary, the Solway Firth, and the hills of the Lake District and Dumfries and Galloway.

Caerlaverock Wetland Centre

The Wildfowl & Wetlands Trust's Caerlaverock reserve near Dumfries is one

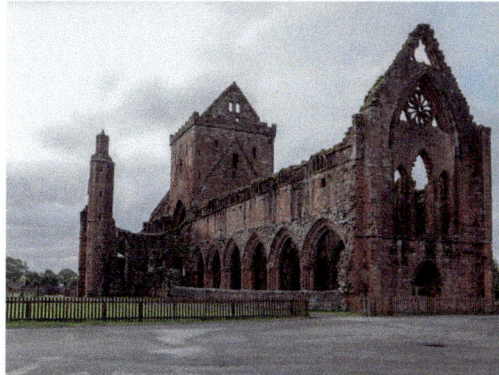

▲ (Top to bottom) Misty view over the Nith Estuary from Criffel; Sweetheart Abbey at New Abbey; A dawn flight of barnacle geese at Caerlaverock Wetland Centre

of the best places to see barnacle geese during their winter stay on the Solway Firth. Most of the barnacle goose population of Norway's Svalbard archipelago flies here from the island of Spitsbergen, with more than forty thousand birds in some years. The numbers have risen steadily from just hundreds a few decades ago.

During the day the birds feed on grassland and saltmarsh alongside the estuary, but at night they rest out on the Solway Firth, necessitating a massed flight from and to the water at sunrise and sunset.

These flights are truly spectacular to see, sometimes with thousands of birds in each group, appearing as silhouettes against the sky. From late autumn to early spring, there are regular guided walks to see this happen that go under the evocative names of 'Dawn Flight' and 'Dusk Flight'.

The reserve lies on the shores of the Solway Firth, just east of the mouth of the Nith Estuary, with areas of grassland and wetlands as well as saltmarsh. It is renowned for the large numbers of swans and ducks that gather here and for the thousands of wading birds that visit in winter, such as dunlins, knots, grey plovers and lapwings.

Birds hides and observation towers provide great opportunities for seeing wildlife and there are wild swan feeds daily from October to March. There is a varied event programme throughout the year and a gift shop too (www.wwt.org.uk/wetland-centres/caerlaverock).

Dumfries to the Mull of Galloway

Further west, the market town of **Castle Douglas** is designated as Scotland's Food Town with a good choice of cafés, restaurants and independent shops.

Kirkcudbright is another popular place to visit, where destinations include the **Stewartry Museum** and 16th century

(Top to bottom) Carsethorn and distant fells from Drumburn viewpoint; 16th century Carsluith Castle near Wigtown ▼

TIDAL BORES ON THE SCOTTISH SHORES

Several tidal bores occur on the Scottish shores of the Solway Firth.

On the Esk a weak wave is sometimes just visible from the shoreline east of Annan. The Nith Tidal Bore is a more impressive sight and in the right conditions forms a low line of surf. Popular viewpoints include the pier at Glencaple and the waterside path at Kingholm Quay. On the best days it makes it as far as the Kirkpatrick Macmillan footbridge just downstream from the centre of Dumfries.

Further west, a much smaller tidal bore forms on the River Bladnoch near Wigtown, where one viewing point is the bird hide at Wigtown Bay Local Nature Reserve, to the southeast of the town.

As discussed earlier, there may only be a few days a year when conditions are suitable for a tidal bore to form, and Chapter 1, Coastal themes, gives tips on water safety and when and where to see them.

The Nith Tidal Bore at Glencaple ▶

◀ The Bladnoch Tidal Bore at Wigtown Bay Local Nature Reserve

MacLellan's Castle. The town has a strong artistic tradition with art galleries and a year-round programme of cultural and arts events.

As in Cumbria, the Scottish shores of the Solway Firth once had several busy ports, including at Annan, Dumfries and Kirkcudbright. In addition to Annan's fishing fleet, Kingholm Quay, Glencaple and Carsethorn near Dumfries were part of its once extensive port and still accommodate leisure craft and a few commercial vessels. Several other harbours and piers around the coastline cater for yachts and pleasure boats.

In contrast, Kirkcudbright remains one of the busiest fishing ports in Scotland, primarily for shellfish, such as scallops. However, the busiest port of all in Dumfries and Galloway is just outside the Solway Firth at Cairnryan near Stranraer, where car ferries depart for Belfast and Larne.

Continuing west, the town of **Wigtown** lies near the Cree Estuary, downstream from the market town of **Newton Stewart**, a popular base for exploring local attractions and the Galloway Hills. In 1998, Wigtown was designated as Scotland's National Book Town and is now a book lover's paradise, hosting Scotland's largest book festival every autumn (www.wigtownbookfestival.com).

It is an interesting place to explore, with cafés, restaurants, and of course many bookshops. **Wigtown Museum** describes the history of the town (www.dgculture.co.uk). Other sights around Wigtown Bay include **Carsluith Castle** and the RSPB's **Crook of Baldoon** Nature Reserve.

The long peninsula of the **Mull of Galloway** marks the end of the Solway Firth (www.mull-of-galloway.co.uk). As at St Bees Head in Cumbria, its spectacular cliffs are a haven for thousands of nesting seabirds from spring to mid-summer, including guillemots, razorbills, fulmars and kittiwakes. Porpoises are sometimes seen too.

Its 19th century lighthouse, now automated, is open to visitors with great views from the top, and includes an exhibition on the history of lighthouses. The **RSPB Visitor Centre** nearby has information on the wildlife, history and geology of the area (www.rspb.org.uk). A coffee house and gift shop perched on a cliff edge provide dramatic views.

Further Reading

Much has been written about the history and wildlife of Morecambe Bay, the Irish Sea and the Solway Firth and the following books, guides, research papers and website links provide many useful insights. The information panels at museums and visitor attractions and the websites listed in the main text were also a great help in researching this guide.

Introduction

Lakeland & Cumbria from the Air, Ronny Mitchell, Halsgrove, Tiverton, 2005
The Cumbria Coastal Way: Morecambe Bay to the Solway Firth, Ian O. Brodie, Krysia Brodie, Cicerone, Milnthorpe, 2007
The England Coast Path: 1,000 Mini Adventures Around the World's Longest Coastal Path, Stephen Neale, Bloomsbury Publishing, London, 2020
The Lake District, Time Out Guides, London, 2010
The Lake District, Lesley Anne Rose, Crimson Publishing, Richmond, 2008
The Outlying Fells of Lakeland, Alfred Wainwright, Chris Jesty (editor), Second edition, Frances Lincoln, 2011 (www.wainwright.org.uk)
Wild Guide Lake District and Yorkshire Dales: Hidden Places, Great Adventures and the Good Life, Daniel Start and Tania Pasco, Wild Things Publishing, Bath, 2016

Chapter 1, Coastal themes

General references

A Guide to Birdwatching in the Lake District and the Coast of Cumbria, David Watson, Photoprint Scotland, 2011
Cumberland shipping in the 18th century, Rupert C. Jarvis, Transactions of the Cumberland & Westmorland Antiquarian & Archaeological Society 54 (series 2). Vol 54, pp. 212-235.
Enjoying the Cumbrian Coast Railway, David John Hindle, Silver Link Publishing Ltd., 2017
Nature Reserves Guide, Cumbria Wildlife Trust (www.cumbriawildlifetrust.org.uk/join)
No Boat Required, Peter Caton, Troubador Publishing, 2011
Ports and Harbours of the North-West Coast, Catherine Rothwell, The History Press, 2010
RSPB Handbook of British Birds, Peter Holden and Richard Gregory, 5th edition, Bloomsbury, 2021
The Geology of the Lake District: an introduction, Robert Westwood, Inspiring Places Publishing, Fordingbridge, 2009
The Ice Age in the Lake District, Alan Smith, The Landscapes of Cumbria No. 3, Rigg Side Publications, Keswick, 2008
The Mersey Estuary: A travel guide, Kevin Sene, Troubador Publishing, 2020
Tidal bores of England, Scotland and Wales, Kevin Sene, Troubador Publishing, 2021
Watching Waterbirds with Kate Humble and Martin McGill, Kate Humble and Martin McGill, Bloomsbury, 2011

Useful websites:

Cumbria Wildlife Trust (www.cumbriawildlifetrust.org.uk)
Hadrian's Wall Country (www.visithadrianswall.co.uk)
Industrial History of Cumbria (www.cumbria-industries.org.uk)
Lake District National Park (www.lakedistrict.gov.uk/learning)
Transactions of the Cumberland & Westmorland Antiquarian Society (www.archaeologydataservice.ac.uk)
Visit Cumbria (www.visitcumbria.com/go; www.visitcumbria.com/towns)

Chapter 2, Morecambe Bay

General references

Along the River Kent, Catherine Rothwell, The History Press, Stroud, 2012
From water to wealth: a self-guided walk around the city of Lancaster, Royal Geographical Society with the Institute of British Geographers, London, 2013 (www.discoveringbritain.org)
Kendal's Port: A maritime history of the Creek of Milnthorpe, Leonard Smith, Lensden Publishing, 2009
No boat required: exploring tidal islands, Peter Caton, Matador Publishing, 2011
Seldom Seen: mapping the hidden assets of Morecambe Bay, Stuart Bastik, Art Gene, Barrow-in-Furness, 2016 (www.morecambebay.org.uk)
The complete guide to the Lancaster Canal, Lancaster Canal Trust, 6th edition, 2012 (www.lctrust.co.uk)
The Gathering Tide: A Journey around the Edgelands of Morecambe Bay, Karen Lloyd, Saraband, Salford, 2016

Useful websites:

Arnside and Silverdale AONB (www.arnsidesilverdaleaonb.org.uk)
Fleetwood Museum (www.fleetwoodmuseum.co.uk)
Grange-over-Sands: Maps, History, Images, Postcards, Nick Thorne, Bodian Photography (www.grangeoversandshistory.weebly.com)
Morecambe Bay Partnership (www.morecambebay.org.uk)
The Dock Museum, Barrow-in-Furness (www.dockmuseum.org.uk)

Chapter 3, Irish Sea

General references

The Duddon Estuary, booklet by English Nature and the Duddon Estuary Partnership
Romans in Ravenglass: Excavation Report 2013-15, K. Hunter-Mann, ArcHeritage/Lake District National Park Authority, 2015
The Port of Ravenglass, Caesar Caine, Transactions of the Cumberland & Westmorland Antiquarian & Archaeological Society 22 (series 2). Vol 22, pp. 101-107, 1922 (includes *Lawson's Chart*)

Useful websites:
Industrial History of Cumbria (www.cumbria-industries.org.uk)
Millom Heritage & Arts Centre (www.millomhac.co.uk)

Chapter 4, Solway Firth
General references
Beach Guide: Scotland's Southern Coast, Solway Firth Partnership (www.solwayfirthpartnership.co.uk)
Dumfries & Galloway, Donald Greig and Darren Flint, Bradt Travel Guides, 2nd edition, 2020
Solway Coast Rambles: Five circular walks around the Roman Frontier, Brian Irving, Hadrian's Wall Trust (www.solwaycoastaonb.org.uk)
Solway's Built Heritage: identifying the distinctive character of the north Solway Plain, Solway Wetlands Landscape Partnership Scheme, Silloth, 2017 (www.solwaycoastaonb.org.uk)
The Fresh and the Salt: The Story of the Solway, Ann Lingard, Birlinn, Edinburgh, 2020
The Solway Coast, H.C. Ivison, Amberley Publishing, Stroud, 2014
The Solway Cumbrian Coast: Beach and explorer's guide, Solway Coast AONB (www.solwaycoastaonb.org.uk)

Useful websites:
Annan Online (www.annan.org.uk)
D&G online (www.dumfries-and-galloway.co.uk)
Solway Coast AONB (www.solwaycoastaonb.org.uk)
Solway Firth Partnership (www.solwayfirthpartnership.co.uk)
Solway Shore-walker (www.solwayshorewalker.wordpress.com)
Solway Wetlands (www.solwaywetlands.org.uk)
The Beacon Museum, Whitehaven (www.thebeacon-whitehaven.co.uk)
Tullie House Museum & Art Gallery (www.tulliehouse.co.uk)

Index

A
accommodation 14-15
  see also tourist information centres
Allonby 164
Annan 188, 189
Arnside 72, 80-81, 83
  Arnside Knott 10, 76, 86
  see also maritime history
Arnside and Silverdale AONB 85-86
  information centre 85
Arnside Knott 10, 76, 86

B
Bardsea 97
Barrow-in-Furness 97, 106-107, 110
  Furness Abbey 5, 34, 104
  The Dock Museum 97
  see also maritime history
Binsey 173
birdwatching *see* waterbirds
Black Combe 18, 127, 143
Bowness-on-Solway 168
  see also Roman presence
Broughton-in-Furness 125
Burgh by Sands 169

C
Caerlaverock
  Caerlaverock Castle 190
  Caerlaverock Wetland Centre 191, 192
canals 35
  Carlisle Canal 35, 179
  Lancaster Canal 35, 65
  Lancaster Canal Trust 65
  Ulverston Canal 35, 105-106
  see also maritime history
Cardurnock Peninsula 166, 167
Cark-in-Cartmel 93
Carlisle 170-172
  Carlisle Canal 179
  Carlisle Castle 171
  Carlisle Cathedral 171
  Tullie House Museum & Art Gallery 171-172
  see also maritime history
Cartmel 74, 75, 80
coastal viewpoints
  Arnside Knott 75-76

Binsey 173
Black Combe 127, 143
Corney Fell 143
Criffel 191
Dunnerholme 124
Hampsfell 75-76
Humphrey Head 74, 75, 76, 88-89
Newtown Knott 143
Sir John Barrow Monument 100, 108
Conishead Priory 96, 97
Criffel 191
Cumbria
  geology 35-37
  habitat 26-32
  see also maritime history
Cumbria Wildlife Trust 29, 86-88, 110-113, 149-150, 183-184
  see also nature reserves and parks, wildlife
cycling
  cycling maps and guides 17
  long distance cycle routes 17, 19
  safety 17
  Sustrans 17

D
dolphins *see* seals, dolphins and porpoises
Drumburgh 169
Duddon Estuary 122-137
Dumfries 190
  Dumfries Museum 190
  Nith Estuary 190-191
  Robert Burns Centre 190
  see also maritime history
Dumfries and Galloway 186-194

E
Eden Valley 174-175
Egremont 121
estuaries
  definition 10
  Duddon Estuary 122-137
  Keer Estuary 66, 68
  Kent Estuary 70-89
  Leven Estuary 90-113
  Lune Estuary 61-63

Nith Estuary 190-191
Ravenglass Estuary 138-151
Solway Firth 152-193
Wyre Estuary 60-61

F
festivals 14
Fleetwood 60
Foulney Island 99, 112-113
Foulshaw Moss 86-88
Furness Abbey 5, 34, 104

G
getting around 15-17
Glasson Dock 61
Grange-over-Sands 75
Gretna Green 188
  Famous Blacksmiths Shop 188

H
habitat 26-32
  Dynamic Dunescapes 30-31
  environmental designations 28
  lowland raised mires 27, 29
  rewilding 31
  sand dunes 30-31
  Wild Ennerdale 32
  see also nature reserves and parks, wildlife
Hadrian's Wall *see* Roman presence
Hampsfell 75-76
Haverigg 126
Haverthwaite 93
  Lakeside & Haverthwaite Railway 93, 94
heritage centres *see* museums
Heysham 66
hillwalking *see* walking
historic sites
  Caerlaverock Castle 190
  Cartmel Priory 75, 81
  Conishead Priory 96, 97
  Crosscanonby Salt Pans 164
  Duddon Iron Furnace 125
  Egremont Castle 121
  Furness Abbey 5, 34, 104
  Holker Hall 93
  Holme Cultram Abbey 167, 176
  King Edward I Monument 169

INDEX | 199

Lancaster Castle 63
Levens Hall 74
Milefortlet 21 164
Muncaster Castle 5, 141
Piel Castle 98, 99, 104
Roman Bath House 147-149
Sizergh Castle 74-75
St Bees Priory 121
St Michael's Church 169, 170
St Patrick's Chapel 66
Sweetheart Abbey 191
see also maritime history
Humphrey Head 74, 76, 88-89

I
Irish Sea 118-121

K
Kent Estuary 70-89
Kirkcudbright 194

L
Lake District 11, 14, 26, 28
   Duddon Valley 128
   Ennerdale 31-32, 121
   Eskdale 142, 144, 145
   geology 35-37
   Grasmere 102
   Kendal 78
   Kentmere Valley 78-79
   Langdale Pikes 104
   Scafell Pike 144
   Ullswater 174
   Wast Water 144, 146
   Windermere 93, 94, 102, 103
Lake District National Park
   Authority 11, 14
Lakeside & Haverthwaite
   Railway 93, 94
Lancashire 58-69
Lancaster 62-65
   Lancaster Castle 63
   Lune Tidal Bore 62
   The Port of Lancaster 65
   Williamson Park 64
   see also maritime history
Lancaster Canal Trust 65
Leven Estuary 90-113
Levens Hall 74
lighthouses 38
   Hodbarrow Lighthouse
      132-133
   Maryport Lighthouse *front*
      cover, 156-157

Mull of Galloway
   Lighthouse 194
Plover Scar Lighthouse 62
Silloth lighthouses 176
St Bees Lighthouse 159, 178
Walney Lighthouse 107, 112
see also maritime history
Lune Estuary 61-63

M
maritime history 32-43
   Barrow-in-Furness 106-107,
      110
   Carlisle 176, 179
   coal mining 36-37, 160-161,
      176-178
   Duddon Iron Furnace 132,
      133
   Dumfries 194
   Fleetwood 60-61
   Greenodd 105
   Harrington 178
   iron ore mining 36-37, 106,
      110, 130
   Lancaster 65
   Maryport 176, 177
   Millom 130, 132-133
   Milnthorpe 80
   Piel Castle, 98, 99
   Port Carlisle 168, 179
   Ravenglass 142, 147-149
   Silloth 176
   Ulverston 105, 108
   Whitehaven 160-161, 178
   Workington 179, 180
   see also canals, lighthouses,
      Roman presence
Maryport 4, 162-164
   Lake District Coast
      Aquarium 162-163
   Maryport Maritime Museum
      163
   Senhouse Roman Museum
      163-164
   see also maritime history
Millom 125, 126, 130
   Millom Heritage & Art
      Centre 126, 130, 133
   see also maritime history
Milnthorpe 74, 80
   see also maritime history
Morecambe 67, 68
Morecambe Bay
   boundaries 57

crossing the sands 81-82, 84
Guide over Sands Trust 84
Rossall Point 60
Walney Lighthouse 107, 112
see also nature reserves and
   parks
Mull of Galloway 194
museums
   Annan Museum 188
   Arnside and Silverdale
      AONB information
      centre 85
   Carnforth Station Heritage
      Centre 16, 68
   Devil's Porridge Museum,
      near Annan 188
   Dumfries Museum 190
   Famous Blacksmiths Shop,
      Gretna Green 188
   Fleetwood Museum 61
   Furness Abbey visitor centre
      104
   Helena Thompson Museum,
      Workington 162
   Heysham Heritage Centre 66
   Lakeland Motor Museum,
      Backbarrow 94
   Lancaster Maritime Museum
      62
   Maryport Maritime
      Museum 163
   Millom Heritage & Art
      Centre 126, 130, 133
   Ravenglass Railway Museum
      142
   Robert Burns Centre,
      Dumfries 190
   Senhouse Roman Museum,
      Maryport 163-164
   Solway Coast Discovery
      Centre, Silloth 166
   The Beacon Museum,
      Whitehaven 160
   The Dock Museum, Barrow-
      in-Furness 97
   The Rum Story, Whitehaven
      161
   Tullie House Museum &
      Art Gallery, Carlisle
      171-172

N
nature reserves and parks
   Caerlaverock Wetland

Centre 191, 192
Campfield Marsh 183-184
Drigg Dunes 151
Duddon Mosses 136-137
Eskmeals Dunes 149-150
Foulshaw Moss 86-87
Hodbarrow 133-136
Humphrey Head 74, 76, 88-89
Leighton Moss 68
Mersehead 191
Mull of Galloway 194
North Walney 112
Roudsea Wood and Mosses 113
Sandscale Haws 136
Siddick Ponds 162
South Walney 110-112
St Bees Head 159, 184-185
Nith Estuary 190-191

P
photography *see* waterbirds
Piel Island 98, 99, 104
porpoises *see* seals, dolphins and porpoises
Port Carlisle 179

R
Ravenglass 33, 140-141
 Muncaster Castle 5, 141
 Ravenglass & Eskdale Railway 141-142
 Ravenglass Railway Museum 142
 see also maritime history
Ravenglass Estuary 138-151
Roa Island 98
Roman presence 32, 34
 Hadrian's Wall 33, 168-169
 Maryport 163-164, 176
 Milefortlet 21 164
 Ravenglass 33, 147-149
 Roman Bath House 147-149
 Senhouse Roman Museum, Maryport 163-164
 Tullie House Museum & Art Gallery, Carlisle 171-172
 see also maritime history
RNLI (Royal National Lifeboat Institution) 20, 23, 66, 98
RSPB (Royal Society for the Protection of Birds) 29,

48, 51, 68, 130, 133-136, 182, 183-185, 191, 194
 see also nature reserves and parks, wildlife

S
safety
 cycling 17
 walking 18
 water 19-22
Scotland 186-194
seals, dolphins and porpoises
 general 43-44
 Sea Watch Foundation 43-44
 South Walney Nature Reserve 43, 110-112
Sea Watch Foundation 43-44
Seascale 121
Seaside visits
 Allonby 164
 Arnside 72, 80-81, 83
 Fleetwood 60
 Grange-over-Sands 75
 Haverigg 125, 126
 Morecambe 67, 68
 Seascale 121
 Silecroft 120
 Silloth 165-166
 St Bees 121
Silecroft 120
Silloth 165-166
Sir John Barrow
 career 108
 Monument 100
Solway Firth 152-194
 boundaries 158
 Mull of Galloway 194
 St Bees Head 159
 see also nature reserves and parks
Solway Coast AONB 183
Solway Coast Discovery Centre, Silloth 166
Source to sea descriptions
 River Duddon 128-129
 River Eden 174-175
 River Esk 144-145
 River Irt 144, 146
 River Kent 78-79
 River Leven 102-103
 River Mite 144
St Bees 121
 St Bees Head 159, 184-185

stone circles 34
 Birkrigg Stone Circle 32, 97
 Swinside Stone Circle 34, 125
steam railways
 Lakeside & Haverthwaite Railway 93, 94
 Ravenglass & Eskdale Railway 141-142
Sunderland Point 65, 66
Sustrans 17

T
tidal bores
 Arnside Bore 40, 41, 83
 Bladnoch Tidal Bore 41
 causes 40
 Duddon Tidal Bore 11, 41, 131
 Leven Tidal Bore 41, 109
 Lune Tidal Bore 41, 62-63
 Nith Tidal Bore 41, 193
 predictions 41
 Solway Bore 41, 180
 tide times 39
 viewpoints 41
 water safety, when watching 41
 Wyre Tidal Bore 41
tourist information centres and websites 14-15

U
Ulverston 95, 96
 Laurel and Hardy Museum 96
 Leven Tidal Bore 109
 Sir John Barrow Monument 108
 Ulverston Canal 96
 see also maritime history

W
walking
 long distance routes 17, 19, 20
 safety 18
 The Ramblers 18
 walking guides and websites 17, 19, 20
Walney Island 99, 110-112, 124
waterbirds 46-51
 barnacle geese 46, 192
 Birdwatchers' Code, the 48, 50
 Cumbria and Lake District species 46, 52-53
 murmurations 49
 Nature Photographers' Code